GW0074646446

How would Jesus vote?

Ram Gidoomal, CBE, is a successful businessman and gives much time to charitable concerns, as well as sitting on a variety of advisory bodies and think tanks. He is a visiting Professor in Entrepreneurship at Middlesex University and an honorary member of the Faculty of Divinity at Cambridge University. His background is South Asian. He was born a Hindu; raised by his uncle as a Sikh; and educated in a Muslim school. He came to Britain with his family as a refugee from East Africa in the 1960s. Several years after arriving in Britain, he became a Christian. He has written a number of books including his autobiography *Sari 'n' Chips*. He and his family live in South London. In 2000 he stood as a candidate for Mayor of London and gained just under 100,000 votes.

David Porter is a professional author, lecturer and broadcaster whose many books include *Back to Basics: the Anatomy of a Slogan*; *With God, For the People* (with Laszlo Tokes, instigator of the Romanian revolution), and *4,000,000 Reasons to Care: How Your Church Can Help the Unemployed* (co-written with Peter Elsom). He has lectured at venues ranging from a Baptist seminary in St Petersburg to the Islamic Academy in Cambridge. A graduate in English Literature, he was also a chartered librarian before becoming a full-time writer. He has a special interest in ethnic issues, children's play and media studies.

'To me it has always been sad that Christians in Britain have often been unable to integrate faith in Jesus with active political argument. The way people vote is so sensitive that it is foolishly argued that the two cannot mix. I am delighted to commend Ram's and David's book as they explore how followers of Jesus might look for his values in the candidates of all parties and choose accordingly. However much we agree with the detail of the argument, the principle is well worth getting to grips with.'

Rt Rev. Graham Dow *Bishop of Carlisle*

'As a Christian minister who has welcomed Ram Gidoomal as a speaker at our church of All Souls, Langham Place, I welcome this book for the luminous contribution it will make in the confusing world of modern politics.'

Rev. Richard Bewes
Rector of All Souls, Langham Place, London W1

'Christians need to think much harder about how their faith should influence their voting decisions. This book helps to clarify the connections.'

Dr Michael Schluter
Director, The Relationships Foundation and author of 'The R Factor'

'Ram Gidoomal has fast become a political icon for Christians all across the UK. His involvement in the London mayoral race brought renewed hope and a breath of fresh air to many Christians in an arena such as politics which has come to be associated with a lack of ethics and morals. This book encourages political responsibility in Christians and shows us how to marry our faith with our civic duties.'

Dr Sola Fola Alade
Pastor, Redeemed Christian Church of God, Chigwell, Essex

'Apathy, cynicism, and political mistrust are the enemies of true democracy. If Christians were denied the vote we would be amongst the first to complain. But how do we vote in such a complex culture? Ram's and David's book will help everyone who cares about where we are heading as a nation.'

Gerald Coates *Pioneer*

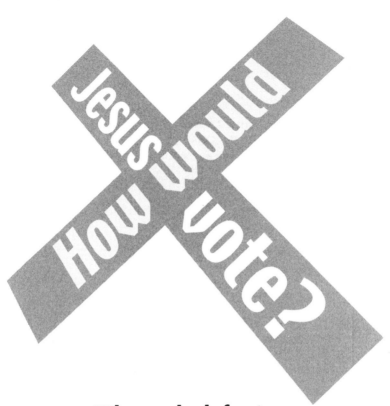

What to look for in your national leaders

RAM GIDOOMAL
WITH DAVID PORTER

MONARCH
BOOKS

Copyright © 2001 by Ram Gidoomal and David Porter.
The right of Ram Gidoomal and David Porter
to be identified as authors of this work has
been asserted by them in accordance with the
Copyright, Design and Patents Act 1988.

First published in the UK in 2001 by Monarch Books.

ISBN 1 85424 541 4

All rights reserved.
No part of this publication may be reproduced or
transmitted in any form or by any means, electronic
or mechanical, including photocopy, recording, or any
information storage and retrieval system, without
permission in writing from Monarch Books,
Concorde House, Grenville Place,
Mill Hill, London NW7 3SA.

Scripture quotations are from the Holy Bible, New International
Version, copyright © 1973, 1978 1984 by the International
Bible Society. Used by permission of Hodder and Stoughton Ltd.

British Library Cataloguing Data
A catalogue record for this book is available
from the British Library.

Designed and produced for the publisher by
Gazelle Creative Productions,
Concorde House, Grenville Place, Mill Hill,
London NW7 3SA.

For Professor Michael Fogarty

Known as 'The Grand Old Man of Democracy in the United Kingdom', Michael Fogarty was for years a source of inspiration and personal support for Ram. It was a great pleasure both for Ram and David when he permitted us to dedicate this book to him.

Sadly, as proofs were about to be returned to the publisher, news came of his death.

This dedication must now serve also as a tribute to an academic whose reputation and circle of friends extended far beyond academia.

Foreword

Over the last ten years Ram Gidoomal has taken a lead in a remarkable variety of enterprises, including Christmas Cracker, South Asian Concern, and a range of think-tanks, advisory groups and regulatory bodies. His background in business and his current experience of the charitable sector, together with his unusual upbringing, have given him the ability to move in many circles. Those of many faiths, and none, regard him as a man of integrity with an independent mind and, above all, as a man who can be trusted. His contribution to modern Britain was recognised recently in the award of the CBE, in honour of his work in combating racism.

During this same period there has been a very significant change in the way most people view politicians. There is mounting cynicism, much of it understandable, for it no longer seems easy to identify a politician with principles. On the other hand, to be fair, the secular atmosphere in which we all live makes it increasingly hard for politicians with faith to make and express a clear link between their faith and their politics. If they do they run the risk that they will be thought to be guilty of electoral manoeuvring at best and, at worst, the risk of not being elected.

Yet the early roots of the Labour party were steeped in non-conformism. A classic exposition of Conservative Party philosophy, written by Quintin Hogg in 1947, defined its core values in specifically Christian terms. It is high time that Christians found their voice again in modern politics.

The current drive for good citizenship fundamentally depends on people participating through the ballot box. If Christians ignore this responsibility, we have no right to complain when society develops along lines that we dislike.

Of course the choices are complex. We live in a fallen world, where compromises and uneasy alliances are often necessary. This is why Ram Gidoomal and David Porter have done us such a service in helping us to ask the right questions. Their impassioned plea not to vote on a single-issue basis is in effect a call to become mature, considered and shrewd as we play our part in contemporary culture.

Politics in the end is about individual people, each of whom can have a moral, social and spiritual influence by their one vote which, together, can change the country. Now is the time to awake to the implications of what is happening in the country at large, to attempt to understand the issues, complex as some of them are, and to act. Ram Gidoomal's insights, experience and sensitivity make this a very important and timely book, not just for Christians but for all of us.

The Reverend Prebendary Sandy Millar,
Vicar, Holy Trinity Brompton

Contents

Preface

Let me explain, as we begin, how this book has come about. I am a businessman who works within the charity and public/voluntary sectors after spending most of my working life as a Director of a multinational niche marketing corporation, the Inlaks Group. Until recently I had little personal experience of the hustings, though I sit on a number of Boards of statutory bodies and am a member of several government-appointed think-tanks, advisory groups and regulatory bodies.

My background is South Asian (by which I mean that my family comes from one of the seven countries in the sub-continent of India). I was born a Hindu; I was raised by my uncle as a Sikh; and I was educated in a Muslim school. I came to Britain with my family as a refugee from East Africa in the 1960s. Several years after arriving in Britain, I became a Christian, a follower of Jesus.[1]

In 2000 I was asked by a newly-formed UK political party, the Christian Peoples Alliance, to be their candidate in the London elections for London Mayor and head their 'top-up' list for seats in the London Assembly. I fought the election, and though I didn't become Mayor and the CPA did not gain seats in the Assembly, the results were encouraging enough to confirm the newly-established party in its decision to fight further elections and establish itself as a new force in British politics.

I am mentioning this at the outset not because the book is a party manifesto – it isn't, and I must emphasise that I am speaking personally in this book. But it's important in any book like this to declare one's interests and explain one's background. The CPA will be mentioned quite often as we go on, but that is because it is the area of politics in which my own practical experience lies. If you would like to know more about the Alliance, I've provided information in an appendix. But you don't need to read it to follow the discussion of the book.

The writing of the book was prompted by an invitation from Tony Collins, Editorial Director of Monarch Publications and publisher of my autobiography, *Sari 'n' Chips*. He pointed out that the British General Election was fast approaching, and that my particular background and mix of experience might provide some intriguing and useful help to those who were attempting to make their minds up about competing political parties, programmes and candidates. The book you are holding in your hands is the result.

Readers of a book with two names on the title page are entitled to know what each of the people named has contributed. *How Would Jesus Vote?* is the latest of several collaborations between myself and David Porter,[2] who is an author and researcher and whose many books include some on political matters (some are included in the Reading List, p. 159). In this book I have contributed the main arguments, and reminiscences of political campaigning are almost always my own, except where David's name is mentioned. The illustrations and anecdotes have been supplied by both of us. David did the actual writing, in close consultation with me, and we have worked together revising the text. David's main material has been transcripts of lengthy conversations between us, his own research, interviews with other people, and other books he has written.

'I' in this book always means Ram Gidoomal: occasionally 'we' is used, indicating that David and I are speaking together.

We both want to acknowledge with gratitude the help of a large number of friends and colleagues, in particular David Campanale, Professor Prabhu Guptara, Deepak Mahtani and Michael Elmer. Our wives, Sunita Gidoomal and Tricia Porter, have helped us to meet a punishing deadline by transcribing tapes and commenting on drafts, and our publisher, Tony Collins, gave us valuable assistance in creating the project, commenting on text and shaping the synopsis. It hopefully goes without saying that any shortcomings of the book are our responsibility, and not that of the people who have helped us!

Anybody writing a book drawing on the tradition of Christian Democracy in Britain owes an enormous debt to the work of David Alton (now Lord Alton), whose founding of the Movement for Christian Democracy with Ken Hargreaves, and campaigning on a range of moral and ethical issues, have been a considerable inspiration to both of us.

Finally, we would both wish to express our appreciation for the interest and support of many people who are members of other faiths, or indeed of none. We have both, for example, enjoyed the hospitality of Islamic organisations where we have appreciated the opportunity of sharing, in an open and courteous environment, what and in whom we believe. I would especially like to thank those in the Muslim, Hindu, Sikh and other faith communities – and many who professed no faith at all – who supported and encouraged me in my London Mayoral campaign. As a South Asian, I would also like to thank numerous members of my extended family and fellow South Asians who, over the years, have helped to sharpen my thinking on the issues discussed in these pages.

Notes

1. See Ram Gidoomal with Mike Fearon, *Sari 'n' Chips* (Monarch, 1993).

2. To prevent possible confusion I should mention that David is an author and editor by profession, and is neither the ex-MP David Porter, nor the Northern Ireland David Porter who has written on political reconciliation!

1
How Would Jesus Vote?

Election time. Through the letterboxes, the promises come.

- ❏ Higher spending on public services...
- ❏ Easing of taxation on essential goods...
- ❏ Taking from the rich to help the poor...
- ❏ Rewarding prudent savers, penalising reckless smokers...
- ❏ Tough on crime...
- ❏ Investment in the local environment...
- ❏ Care for the elderly, protection for children, opportunities for young people...
- ❏ Vote for me! Vote for me! Vote for me! For I will deliver...

The faces on the manifestos are often unfamiliar: candidates given an opportunity by their party to gain experience campaigning against a sitting MP, independents riding a hobby horse, sometimes the bizarre and the frankly weird. And when the faces are familiar, how much do we really know about them? How can we be sure that these people will really represent us in the House of Commons, in the Regional Assembly, in the District Council, in the Parish Council? If we elect them, how will they use their power in the issues that really matter to us?

Most of us regard voting as a privilege and a responsibility. People chained themselves to railings, sometimes even gave their lives for us to have the vote. As I write, the American nation is having a dramatic demonstration of the significance of individual votes, as the long weeks of recounts and recriminations following the 2000 Presidential election slowly wind to a conclusion after lengthy wrangles over a few hundred votes.

Our votes matter, and when a significant number of people decide that they don't matter, and don't bother to vote in an election, political commentators regard the low turnout as a meaningful factor in the outcome.

But how should we use our vote? Should we vote for the party we've always voted for, perhaps on the principle that they haven't entirely messed things up, and better the devil we know? Or should we select an untried, inexperienced unknown who talks a good election – but who's to know how he or she will perform if elected? Maybe we should choose on the basis of some key point that for us is the most important issue in politics – so important, in fact, that we would never dream of voting for somebody who disagreed with us on that issue. But what about candidates who do agree with us on that issue, but seem to be completely at sea on most other matters? Even more, what do we do if *two* candidates happen to agree with us about our personal key issue?

I expect many readers of this book are Christians. What difference should that make? Indeed, what difference should it make if one has a religious faith of any kind? Theologians and philosophers have often argued that the Church has its own sphere of authority and so does the State, and that the two should not trespass on each other's territory. 'What has Athens to do with Jerusalem?' demanded Tertullian, the African lawyer who, writing in the early centuries of the Church, became known as one of its fathers. Athens was the centre of the Greek cultural world, Jerusalem the city that stood at the centre of the Christian world.

> What concord is there between the Academy and the Church? What between heretics and Christians?... With our faith, we desire no further belief.[3]

But that does not mean, and certainly did not mean for Tertullian, that Christians should leave the state to get on with things, with no input or criticism from the church. But what kind of relationship should there be between the two?

For followers of Jesus, wisdom and maturity are defined in the Bible very simply. They mean becoming more like him. That was how Paul spoke of his own journey to maturity.

> I want to know Christ and the power of his resurrection and the fellowship of sharing in his sufferings, becoming like him in his death, and so, somehow, to attain to the resurrection from the dead. Not that I have already obtained all this, or have already been made perfect, but I press on to take hold of that for which Christ Jesus took hold of me. (Philippians 3:10–12)

He spoke of himself as an imitator of Christ, as one who was seeking to be more like him. The New Testament has a lot to say about the 'mind of Christ' and how to develop that mind in ourselves. It's not a matter of second-guessing God, but of dedicating one's spiritual life to becoming more and more like him so that when making choices or decisions, increasingly one will become aware of what God's view of the matter might be.

That is why this book has the title, *How Would Jesus Vote?* We believe that the world of secular, material politics is important to God. Of course there were no elections in Jesus' Palestine that looked anything like our modern Western democratic processes, and there are no records of Jesus having voted for anything at all. But there is ample evidence that Jesus, when he lived as a man and was a resident of an earthly state, took a very keen interest in what the government was doing and was not afraid to criticise earthly powers. So in this book I want to consider what might have been his criteria and approach towards modern elections. Faced with competing manifestos and candidates, how would he decide how to cast his vote? What would be the major non-negotiables, and what would be the areas where compromise was acceptable or which were not of great importance? How *would* Jesus vote?

Jesus at the Polls

The notion of Jesus voting might seem distinctly odd. Some might even find it quite offensive. A bizarre picture easily comes to mind that's hard to get rid of – a Holman-Hunt style Jesus, wearing shining robes and a halo, his brunette hair long and curling. He cuts an incongruous figure, black-lead pencil in hand, standing in a plywood booth in some school or community hall. He is perusing the list of candidates that's pinned up next to the electoral regulations that nobody ever reads. A black tin box, secured with string and sealing wax, awaits his completed voting slip.

For many of us, Jesus doesn't belong in that world at all.

But if Jesus had been born two millennia after he actually was born, nobody would have recognised him as he walked among us, any more than the people of his own time knew, just from looking, that Jesus son of Joseph the carpenter was actually the saviour of the world. Seeing him standing in a polling booth would have raised nobody's eyebrows, because Jesus would look like every other voter: a normal twenty-first-century person in twenty-first-century clothes, doing one of the necessary tasks of twenty-first-century citizenship.

So the real question is not what Jesus looks like in a polling booth, but what is he doing? How would Jesus vote? How would he choose among competing candidates? Would he vote along party lines, and if so, what party would get his vote? And behind all those questions there's another question: *Would* Jesus vote?

I am so convinced that the answer to the last question is 'Yes' that I have relegated it to an appendix (p. 147), in which I have briefly discussed why I believe that Jesus would have voted, and why he would expect us to vote. For me the question of *how* he would vote is far more important, and it's that question which we will be thinking about in this book.

Christians in Britain

For some readers who have picked this book up out of curiosity, the title might seem odd for a different reason.

Nobody knows exactly how many Christians there are in Britain. Estimates vary widely. Of course it depends on what you mean by 'Christian'. The most generous estimates are based on Census returns, but – as the following extract from a Parliamentary debate suggests – you have to handle such figures with care.

> The organisation Christian Research estimates that 65 per cent of the UK is Christian and that non-Christian religion comprise 8 per cent, with at least 27 per cent of the country being agnostic. That information is available already, before the need for a census. It leads to the very important point made by the National Secular Society, that if, for example, the census shows that 65 per cent have indicated that they

are Christian, one could get an inflated idea of the numbers of religious adherents. There is a very big difference between being a member of a particular religion and a follower of that religion... With the Church's attendance falling rapidly, those ticking the 'none' box could quite conceivably be the largest category. It would be interesting to compare those professing to have a religion with attendance at places of worship.[4]

In global terms, the *UK Christian Handbook* estimates that 28.3% of the world's population identified themselves as Christians in 1990, and expects this to drop to 27.7% by the year 2000 and to 27.1 in 2010 – the drop being accounted for by lower birth rates among Christians than among some other religions.[5] On the other hand, the US Center for World Mission estimated three years ago that the total number of Christians in the world is fairly stable at between 30% and 35%, rising by around 2.3% per annum, about the same rate as the world's population.[6]

Yet whether the figures show a slight decline or a slight increase, Christians are not a majority community in the world. Nor, after adjusting for nominal Christianity and disallowing those who register as 'Christian' instinctively without thinking, are they a majority in Britain. The *UK Christian Handbook* estimates the total church membership of Britain at 5,861,796, out of a total population that was estimated in 1997 at just under 59,000,000. (It is worth putting such statistics into a context, however. For example, though church membership has declined by 21% since 1980, membership of trade unions declined by 55% over the same period.)[7]

Interested parties

So it would be reasonable for any reader who is not a committed follower of Jesus to ask why on earth they should be interested to know how Jesus would vote – or why, in Britain's modern pluralist society, they should be expected to read a book written by Christians and arguing from a Christian perspective.

I would like to suggest three reasons.

First, *Christians believe that all human beings are made in the image of God and are of inestimable value in God's eyes.* The New Testament teaches an ethical and moral agenda that sometimes seems almost beyond the capability of human beings to put into practice. The Sermon on the Mount has been an inspiration to countless people who would not consider themselves Christians, including the great Indian leader Mahatma Gandhi. Christian ideals fired the early Labour Party; and when in 1947 Quintin Hogg (later Lord Hailsham of Marylebone) wrote a classic exposition of Conservative Party philosophy,[8] he defined its core in terms of religious commitment and he defined it in specifically Christian terms.

The gospel of Jesus enshrines values that have not always been implemented as they should have been; but when those values have been taken seriously they have transformed whole societies. Jesus preached the value of humility, of self-denying love, of inverting the social order so that the least became first and the greatest became the least. He championed the disadvantaged and the vulnerable. Women had dignity in his presence and children were drawn to him. He attacked greed and exploitation and welcomed sinners to eat with him. There have been some disgraceful, tragic episodes in the history of Christianity – but they were episodes when Christians lost sight of Jesus.

Biblical Christianity has a social responsibility as well as an evangelistic responsibility. Theologian Dr Carl Henry observed,

> Evangelical Christians have a message doubly relevant to the present social crisis... For they know *the God of justice and of justification*... Whenever Christianity has been strong in the life of a nation, it has had an interest in both law and gospel, in the state as well as the church, in jurisprudence and in evangelism.[9]

A religion whose followers are commanded to live in the light of such values naturally attracts interest in its Founder. And it's especially interesting to consider what the Founder of such a religion would have thought important when choosing which political programme, candidate or party to support. That is why I have written this book, and I hope you will find the subject as challenging and interesting as I have found it.

Second, *Christians represent a substantial part of the history and culture of the British people*. It's true, of course, that Britain is no longer a 'Christian country' in the sense that you are not going to find most people sitting in church each Sunday. But British law, government and local administration, and much else, are all derived from Christianity. If you want to understand the British political process, it's important to have some understanding of how the Bible discusses society and government (and wider moral and ethical issues as well).

But more than that, Christianity in Britain represents a bulwark of faith. For those who are not Christians, it occupies ground that might otherwise be occupied by forces that are much less concerned about the worth of human beings and the value of the individual. That was the experience of citizens of communist countries during the post-war years. In Hungary, for example, after the revolutions of 1989, the new government turned to the church for help in its welfare and relief projects. For decades the church had been one of the few agencies doing such work. At great personal cost and risk its members had fed, sheltered and nurtured those who had no place in the totalitarian state.

The Roman Catholic cardinal, John Newman, once commented memorably, 'The Church of England is a protection against heresies greater than itself'. He was making a gentle criticism of Anglicanism, from which he was the nineteenth century's most famous convert, but the point has a wide application. In that sense, the Christian faith is a protector of other faiths, and once again, the views of its Founder on what constitutes good government and good social order have a much wider relevance than just to its own membership.

Third, *Christianity is a religion of the spirit. It stands opposed to materialist and anti-human forces.* In a sense, what happens to followers of Jesus is a straw in the wind for religions as a whole. If Christianity is attacked, other religions are vulnerable on the same grounds. Even if you are not a follower of Jesus you should be taking an interest in what happens to Christianity. Maybe you disagree profoundly with the Christian gospel – yet you and Christianity have some common cause.

> They came for the Communists, and I didn't object,
> Because I was not a Communist;
> They came for the Socialists, and I didn't object,
> Because I was not a Socialist;
> They came for the union leaders, and I didn't object,
> Because I wasn't a labour leader;
> They came for the Jews, and I didn't object,

Because I was not a Jew;

Then they came for me, and there was no one left to object.

Those words were written by Martin Niemöller, who was a Lutheran theologian and leading anti-Nazi resistance fighter. A U-Boat commander in the First World War, in the Second he joined the Confessing Church, which opposed the Nazi government. For this he was arrested in 1937 and until 1945 was imprisoned in Sachsenhausen and Dachau.

The Mind of Christ

I have already suggested that talking about how Jesus would vote means attempting to analyse Jesus' mind. For a Christian that might seem impertinent, and for somebody who is not, it might seem impossible. How can you possibly enter into the thought-processes of a historical figure who lived 2000 years ago – whether you believe him to be the Saviour of the world or not?

Some people have tried to do just that in a very simplistic way. In 1948 an American writer, Charles Sheldon, published a novel called *In His Steps*,[10] which became a best-seller. It was the story of a community, the American township of Raymond, that was transformed by the application of a simple question to every issue, however complex. The question was, 'What would Jesus do?' From small beginnings the message spread throughout the town, and a new ethos of piety and morality replaced the self-centred and dishonest lifestyle of the old Raymond. The book ended in visionary fashion, with the dream of what had happened in Raymond going on to transform America and beyond that the entire world.

I have found myself that asking the question 'What would Jesus do/say/argue?' has been very helpful in all sorts of situations, for example when preparing for TV interviews and public meetings. It's been a valuable tool with which to identify priorities and check my own attitudes. Few of us, scrutinising the way that we think and act according to that powerful searchlight, will emerge without change. It's a method I would recommend to anybody.

But the curious thing about *In His Steps* is the way the question is asked. The story doesn't read like the stories of the great Christian revivals of the past. The appeal to what Jesus would do is expressed almost wholly in ethical and moral terms, and the teachings of Jesus are presented almost as a better business plan. There certainly is no sign of the wholesale repentance and conversion of an entire community, of the kind that swept Welsh towns and American cities in the great revivals of the twentieth century. 'What would Jesus do?' simply leads to lifestyles that work better than those that Raymond had adopted before.

There is a sense in which Sheldon was quite right: the ethics of the New Testament do lead to better relationships, a higher integrity, a more compassionate society. Whether or not you acknowledge Jesus as Lord and Saviour, his teachings do benefit those who practise them. However, that isn't Christianity. And it falls very short of discerning the mind of Jesus. It's simply a biblically-influenced moral code.

Broadening the Question

Take, for example, the issue of money – a very important part of life in Jesus' day, just as it is in ours. Jesus talks about it a lot in the Bible.

Many Christians would say that money *per se* isn't an issue, nor is wealth, nor is the economy. They would say that what a Christian ought to be concerned about is the issues that Jesus raised: and the majority of his references to money in Scripture are to do with having enough of it or having too little. So if our brother or sister has too little money and we have more than we need, we should do what Jesus would do: we should give some of our surplus cash to our needy brother or sister.

That, of course, is a good thing to do, and you can build a set of philanthropic moral principles around such charitable giving that will certainly make the world a better place. But a thoughtful reading of the Bible shows that if we think that this is *all* that was going on in Jesus' mind – a simple restoration of material equality – we are missing a great deal. Jesus doesn't talk about money in isolation as a problem detached from the rest of life, one that can be solved by generosity. Look for example at the parable of the Good Samaritan. A great many issues are raised in that story. British Prime Minister Margaret Thatcher addressed some of them on 21 May 1988 when she addressed the General Assembly of the Church of Scotland.[11] She introduced her speech by saying, 'Perhaps it would be best if I began by speaking personally as a Christian, as well as a politician, about the way I see things'. She made some interesting comments, such as her interpretation of 2 Thessalonians 3:10 – 'If a man will not work, he shall not eat', which she took as proof that 'We are told we must work and use our talents to create wealth'. Building on this rather unusual exegesis she went on to explain that 'it is not the creation of wealth that is wrong but the love of money for its own sake', again making rather surprising use of the tenth commandment to support her case and using a quotation from C. S. Lewis that not everybody will accept in this context.

The speech was described sceptically by Rachel Tingle as

'a moral and biblical defence of [Margaret Thatcher's] policies'.[12] Most people agreed that this was the speech's main purpose, but unfortunately Lady Thatcher missed the point of the parable. For her, the two pence that the Samaritan provided for the victim's accommodation and care were a justification of the trickle-down economy; her exposition turned into a discussion of who had wealth and who had not, and the desirability of accumulating wealth. But the issues can't be coerced in that way, and Jesus, to judge by the challenge he threw out to his listeners at the end of the parable, appears to have had a different point in mind.

He refused to reduce the difficult issue of money down to a few simple rules. He told us that man should not live by bread alone; he endorsed the payment of taxes to Caesar. He did not condemn the Samaritan for having money, but he clearly didn't suggest that the payment of two pence to the inn-keeper had established economic parity between the Samaritan and the wounded traveller. And the story has other reverberations. Issues are raised in the parable that are relevant to the National Health Service. There are also some implications for road safety, and policing. Admittedly it's easy to read too much into a parable that was intended to make a simple point, but Jesus is telling the story and the details reflect some of his concerns. For Jesus, charity was not a simple, single act. It was a complex deed that triggered repercussions in many other areas of life for both the one who gave and the one who received.

And as we evaluate the policies of politicians, we should beware of reducing our analysis down to simple factors. We should be considering what the impact of the proposed policies will be, and how they will affect other, perhaps less visible matters. If large spending on one social need is promised, does that mean there will be cutbacks elsewhere?

If a particular group is singled out for increased benefits, job opportunities and other improvements, does that deprive other groups of the same advantages? Is an act of charity also a failure of social justice?

It's been said that a fool is a person who knows the cost of everything and the value of nothing. Jesus was constantly aware of the implications of the choices people made, and the dangers of limited thinking. He always opened out issues, never closed them up. And he handed out very few easy answers. To do so would have been to engage in 'single-issue' politics. In Section 4, we look at some of the implications of going that route.

How would Jesus think?

Discerning the mind of Jesus is something about which the Bible actually has a great deal to say. As we come to the end of this first section I want to look briefly at some Bible passages, not to discern at this point Jesus' views on voting and politics, but to explore the biblical teaching about the mind of Jesus.

Growth

> Therefore, I urge you, brothers, in view of God's mercy, to offer your bodies as living sacrifices, holy and pleasing to God – this is your spiritual act of worship. Do not conform any longer to the pattern of this world, but be transformed by the renewing of your mind. Then you will be able to test and approve what God's will is – his good, pleasing and perfect will. (Romans 12:1–2)

This passage talks about transformation through 'the renewal of the mind'. It's interesting that Paul does not regard being able to test things by the yardstick of God's 'good, pleasing and perfect will' (in other words, being so aware of how God sees an issue that you will be able to test whether something or some course of action conforms to God's will) as an optional extra. For Paul it's part of growing; you can't be a mature disciple of Jesus without being transformed in this way. Be transformed – *then* you will be able to test. It's a step you can't omit.

But maturity doesn't happen overnight and there is no optimum speed at which Christians grow in their faith. The renewing of the mind is a continuous process. Part of that process is learning to look at things with new eyes. How does a manifesto, a political party, a candidate, look when viewed with new, Christ-inspired eyes? How do they look when measured against the benchmark of biblical principles? We might even adopt a utilitarian approach and ask, 'How far would this manifesto, party or candidate advance the cause of the values of Jesus and Christian freedoms?'

In this book I will be arguing that there is no one way for a Christian to vote. There is no party for which every right-thinking, well-taught Christian should vote – not even the Christian Peoples Alliance! I can't give you a list of Christian candidates who automatically deserve your Christian vote, and I can't give you a list of policies such that a candidate offering 70% of them or more is the candidate you should vote for.

What I want to share in this book is my conviction that if we want to vote according to how Jesus would vote, we should think, and think biblically, and then vote, knowing that we have chosen prayerfully, thoughtfully and biblically. If that's the case then it doesn't matter that our Christian friend or neighbour, voting in the same election, votes for a different candidate or party than the one we voted for.

Service

> Your attitude should be the same as that of Christ Jesus:
> Who, being in very nature God, did not consider equality
> with God something to be grasped, but made himself noth-
> ing, taking the very nature of a servant, being made in
> human likeness. And being found in appearance as a man,
> he humbled himself and became obedient to death – even
> death on a cross! Therefore God exalted him to the highest
> place and gave him the name that is above every name, that
> at the name of Jesus every knee should bow, in heaven and
> on earth and under the earth, and every tongue confess that
> Jesus Christ is Lord, to the glory of God the Father.
> (Philippians 2:5–10)

Humility is a hallmark of the mind of Jesus. The King of
the universe set aside his kingship and became a man, born
into a humble family with none of the trappings of royalty,
far less of divinity.

I believe that this passage from Paul's letter to the
Philippian church has major significance for Christians
involved in politics, either as voters or as politicians. The
world is full of political leaders who have risen to the top
out of ambition and pushed other people out of the way
because they wanted the power and prestige of political
office more than anything else in the world. You can see it
in innumerable newsreels from different parts of the world:
politicians who are clearly enjoying their job for all the
wrong reasons.

'Wrong', that is, when measured by the searching bench-
test of passages like this one. Jesus taught and practised service. He was prophesied as the Suffering Servant, and in his
life he demonstrated his desire to serve, both by what he
said and what he did: in washing his disciples' feet, in small

matters like helping his disciples put their nets where the fish were shoaling, and supremely in the act of atonement itself, his crucifixion. He spelled out this aspect of his ministry in a specific reference to government:

> A dispute arose among them as to which of them was considered to be greatest. Jesus said to them, 'The kings of the Gentiles lord it over them; and those who exercise authority over them call themselves Benefactors. But you are not to be like that. Instead, the greatest among you should be like the youngest, and the one who rules like the one who serves. For who is greater, the one who is at the table or the one who serves? Is it not the one who is at the table? But I am among you as one who serves.' (Luke 22:24–27).

Whom should we vote for, if we want to vote as Jesus would vote? Passages like the ones I have quoted above – and there are many similar passages in the Bible – make it plain that we should be very careful about voting for any candidate who gave the impression that his motive for seeking office was anything other than a desire to serve. It's possible to imagine situations in which it might be right to vote for such a candidate, but there would have to be very compelling reasons to overlook such a clear contradiction of Jesus' criterion for good government.

Guidance

> The Spirit searches all things, even the deep things of God. For who among men knows the thoughts of a man except the man's spirit within him? In the same way no-one knows the thoughts of God except the Spirit of God. We have not received the spirit of the world but the Spirit who is from God, that we may understand what God has freely given us. This is what we speak, not in words taught us by human wis-

dom but in words taught by the Spirit, expressing spiritual truths in spiritual words. The man without the Spirit does not accept the things that come from the Spirit of God, for they are foolishness to him, and he cannot understand them, because they are spiritually discerned. The spiritual man makes judgments about all things, but he himself is not subject to any man's judgment: 'For who has known the mind of the Lord that he may instruct him?' But we have the mind of Christ. (1 Corinthians 2:10–16)

I have left this passage until last, because it makes a point with which I would like to end this chapter. Voting is a complex matter. Often, as we shall see in the pages that follow, we just don't know enough about a situation to arrive at an objective answer purely from the facts known to us. Is it right to support a move to build a factory that will create hundreds of jobs, but will cause local business blight and also environmental damage? Should we vote for a programme of reform that will force a large number of people into relocation and different employment markets? Is it right to vote for legalisation of a drug that will be pushed underground if it remains illegal?

There are many, many issues like these, moral and ethical quandaries in which we simply don't have the information or the expertise to make a decision. In voting for a candidate, we sometimes have to leave parts of the manifesto unexplored because we're not competent to evaluate the candidate's promises.

In such cases, Christians believe they have a resource that is helpful in all complex decisions. To have the mind of Christ, in this sense, means that we have access to God himself through Jesus Christ, and through prayer we can ask for guidance.

Does that take the responsibility of thinking through

political manifestos away from us? It doesn't. The Bible never endorses a fire-and-forget approach to prayer. But countless Christians have described how prayer has clarified issues that previously they found difficult and complex. Sometimes prayer helps in making difficult political decisions – for voters, this may mean for example breaking family and personal links with a party they have grown up with, and facing personal criticism for doing so. Politics is full of hard choices and difficult situations, whether you are Prime Minister or just a name on the electoral register.

But it was a core element in Jesus' thinking that difficult decisions did not have to be taken alone. In the Gospels we frequently find him at prayer, sometimes in what seem to be his customary prayer-times and sometimes at moments of deep personal crisis.

How would Jesus vote? In this book we will be looking at a number of elements that would be part of his thinking. Prayer, without a doubt, would be indispensable to all of them.

Notes

3. Tertullian, *The Prescription Against Heretics*, VII.

4. House of Commons, *Hansard*, Debates for 20 June 2000, Col. 286.

5. Quoted in *Religion Today*, Current News Summary, 19 October 1999.

6. Greg H. Parsons, Executive Director, US Center of World Mission: quoted in Zondervan News Service 1997.

7. Peter Brierley (ed.), *UK Christian Handbook 2000–2001* (Christian Research, 1999).

8. Quintin Hogg, *The Case for Conservatism* (Penguin, 1947).

9. Quoted by John R. W. Stott, *The Contemporary Christian* (IVP, 1992), p. 338.

10. Charles M. Sheldon, *In His Steps* (Henry E. Walter, 1948), p. 236.

11. The full text of her speech is included as an Appendix in: Michael Alison and David L. Edwards (eds), *Christianity and Conservatism* (Hodder & Stoughton, 1990), p. 333.

12. Rachel Tingle, *Another Gospel? An Account of the Growing Involvement of the Anglican Church in Secular Politics* (Christian Studies Centre, 1988), p. 9.

2
Making Choices

Wouldn't it be nice if the Bible contained a handy supplement with exact instructions on how to make all major decisions, and a list of the views we ought to have on all the important issues of life?

Well, yes – and no.

No, because we would turn into robots. Our minds would become largely redundant and our 'Christian minds', in the sense we discussed the term in the last chapter, would be superfluous.

Yes, because it would certainly make life a lot simpler.

For example it would be extremely useful, in today's Britain, to be able to look up 'beggars, giving to', and get instant guidance. But in real life the situation is very complex. 'That beggar you walked past in the High Street the other day seemed to be needy and hungry.' – But didn't you read somewhere that a lot of beggars make a very good living? – 'What if I give him money and he just spends it on drink?' On the other hand, did you *really* need the cup of coffee on which you spent your loose change ten minutes later? – 'Maybe I ought to have talked to him about Jesus.' But didn't he look as if he needed a hot meal more than he needed a sermon? – 'Ah, but if I just feed him I'm encouraging him in his begging'...

There are no cut-and-dried answers, no little book in which you can look up 'beggar' and know exactly what to do. Read the Bible and it asks *you* questions: questions like 'Who is my neighbour?' Watch Jesus dealing with people in need and you discover that he didn't have a stock response that he produced every time the same kind of situation came up. Sometimes sick and dying people came to him and he healed them: he restored their sight, cured their haemorrhages, made them walk again. But there's that curious incident in Mark's Gospel, where Jesus seems to have turned his back on a whole township of needy cases and simply gone off somewhere else:

> That evening after sunset the people brought to Jesus all the sick and demon-possessed. The whole town gathered at the door, and Jesus healed many who had various diseases. He also drove out many demons, but he would not let the demons speak because they knew who he was.
>
> Very early in the morning, while it was still dark, Jesus got up, left the house and went off to a solitary place, where he prayed. Simon and his companions went to look for him, and when they found him, they exclaimed: 'Everyone is looking for you!'
>
> Jesus replied, 'Let us go somewhere else – to the nearby villages – so that I can preach there also. That is why I have come.' (Mark 1:32–38)

When you read the passage in context you realise why Jesus made this apparently strange decision. It was a matter of priorities. Jesus did not come to heal a small number of local invalids. He did heal, but that was not his main task. Faced with an overwhelming need he made a difficult choice. But it must have been incomprehensible to the disciples: 'Lord, the sick are coming in their hundreds, the ambulances are arriving as we speak!'

And Jesus replied, 'Let's find some other village to go to.'

Making choices according to how Jesus would choose in the same situation doesn't absolve us from using our minds. We might be making personal, practical life-choices. We might be deciding where we stand on ethical and moral issues. We might just be pondering one of those situations where a wrong answer won't exactly be earth-shattering, but it would be nice to have a short cut to the right answer. Whatever the situation facing us, it is very unlikely to have an immediate, unquestionable answer. We're almost always going to have to think.

Some people have assumed that God is like a celestial chocolate machine: you put in your prayer, and out pops the answer to your question. But the Jesus we see in the Gospels had a very different way of handling people's questions and problems. He did not always give brief, succinct answers needing no further discussion. He habitually forced his listeners to confront the implications of their own questions and work out answers for themselves. When his opponents tried to compromise him by tricking him into a treasonable statement about Caesar, he set them a tricky conundrum of his own, to do with coins and tribute (*cf* Luke 20:20–25). At his own arrest, he submitted – and by the words with which he did so, he forced his captors to admit the illegality of the whole proceedings (Luke 22:52–53). He often answered a question with a question of his own, or appeared to ignore the question completely, although what he went on to say invariably answered it with far more depth than the questioner had bargained for and sometimes showed up the limitations of the original question. People who talked to Jesus must still, hours and days afterwards, have been thinking about what he said to them.

Britain's Pluralist Society

Much of Jesus' conversation was with people who shared his Jewish background, and their questions were set against that backdrop: questions that asked who Jesus was, what he was doing, and what he had to say about Old Testament teaching and the authority of the Jewish leaders.

As we saw in Chapter 1, today's Britain does not have a Christian consensus any more. If it did, half the chat shows and discussion programmes on TV would disappear and the other half would be very dull. We live in a pluralist society.

A pluralist society necessarily has to be a pragmatic society. Politicians have to represent and serve a wide range of different people groups and their interests; which is why politics has been called 'the art of the possible', a description that quite rightly sets off alarm bells in thoughtful Christian minds. Britain has a wonderful Christian heritage, and Christians are not the only people who acknowledge that much of the strength and quality of British life today derives from it.

But we saw in Chapter 1 that we are not a 'Christian' society in any statistical sense, and to legislate as if we were would be to destroy the civil and sometimes the human rights of millions of British citizens who are Christian neither by national nor ethnic background. Sometimes a kind of double standard affects Christians. We protest, as we should, at abuses of Christian citizens' freedom in, for example, certain Hindu or Islamic fundamentalist states. Yet at the same time we are tempted to feel that our Christian heritage in Britain requires that we should use the law to penalise people who refuse to be converted to

Christianity, or at least decline to behave like Christians. The Old Testament has a lot to say on the treatment of aliens within one's borders, and Britain is not the only country in the world with a patchy record on this issue.

Pluralism in politics opens up some intriguing issues. If it is the case, as I'm sure it is (and I have campaigned on this very basis), that a Christian politician can present policies that somebody who is not a Christian could feel able to endorse and vote for, then the reverse is just as feasible: a thoughtful Christian may well find him or herself voting for a candidate of a different religion, or none at all, and rejecting an explicitly Christian candidate, after evaluating policies with a sincere attempt to apply the mind of Jesus.

It's an option, and probably one that won't often be available. It might be a way forward, for example, if the candidate or candidates fight on a manifesto that is dominated by a profoundly Christian single issue, such as pro-life issues, or issues in education, or legislation on sexual matters, but is badly thought out and barely Christian in all its other proposals. My colleague David Porter recalls a local election when he was living in Liverpool: though there were no explicitly Christian candidates, the party he normally voted for offered only one tangible local policy – to get the gypsy travellers moved on from Liverpool. The other major parties were offering rhetoric but nothing that applied directly to the local situation. The communist candidate, on the other hand, had a well-thought-out analysis of local problems and practical plans to deal with them. For the first and last time in his life, David voted communist, a decision he still looks back on with some astonishment. Yet viewed in terms of local problems, the communist candidate was the only one who seemed to be able and willing to serve the community and deal with people's real concerns.

That's probably a (literally) once-in-a-lifetime option, but it illustrates the point well!

Christians will sometimes find it difficult to support explicitly Christian politicians who are people of great faith but are not very good at being politicians. In some of the Eastern European countries, governments with a strong Christian element were voted into power when communism collapsed. They had a mandate to govern the spiritual as well as the material needs of the people. But as time went by, it became obvious that they were only good at governing the spiritual side of the nation. The national economy meanwhile deteriorated, quality of life diminished, there was a failure of progress towards building links with the outside world. In some cases, the result was that a version of communism or left-wing socialism again became a force in the country. This, for example, was what happened in Hungary.

Another example might be US President Jimmy Carter, whose memoirs of his time in office, *Keeping Faith*, reveal him to be a man of huge integrity, apparently uninterested in promoting his own image or glorifying his presidency in any way.[13] Carter's decision-making was guided by solid biblical principles, and he is quite open in his memoirs, as he was when president, about the fact that he drew strength and inspiration from prayer, Bible-reading and his church. Yet many American Christians voted against his re-election on the grounds that they believed him to be an ineffective president, or at least the wrong president for America's needs at the time.

A third situation where Christians might feel unable to vote for Christian politicians is when they disagree with how those politicians apply Christianity to politics. They expect a Christian politician in office to behave in a certain way and to do his or her work in a certain way and are, rightly or wrongly, disappointed. The problem in such cases comes down to a difference of opinion over what 'doing politics Christianly' means, or sometimes over whether religion should be involved in politics at all. A current example is Tony Blair, who throughout his time as British Prime Minister has quietly and visibly shown himself to be a church-goer and a man of strong faith, but has not sought to articulate 'biblical politics'. For that reason, rightly or wrongly, some Christians have found it difficult to see him as a force for Christianity in politics.

A Matter of Principle

So the question 'How would Jesus vote?' can't be answered simply by saying, 'By voting for politicians who believed in him.' (Even if it could, matters would become confused again as soon as two committed Christian candidates stood as candidates in the same election!)

I want to suggest, too, that in our pluralist society, voting responsibly means voting for candidates who will represent the interests of, and fairly govern, the largest possible number of the different groups that make up British society, whether or not those people voted for that candidate. Naturally, a Christian voter will bring a further set of criteria to bear: there are some political parties he or she could not vote for (a party whose manifesto included a pledge to outlaw Christianity would be an obvious example of such a party). But even so, it is clear from our discussion so far that a cross-section of people seriously thinking through the same candidate list asking 'How would Jesus vote?' will not arrive at anything like a unanimous verdict.

How then should we vote?

Let's think for a moment about how we make any choice

where the options are complex. Choosing a candidate or party, or deciding whether to vote for or against a government policy in a referendum or similar national vote, essentially means choosing the option that satisfies the greatest number of items on one's personal list of criteria. Cynics might call it 'choosing the least worst option', but in fact we make a great many decisions that way.

Consider how we choose our career. What matters most to us? Job satisfaction will be high on anybody's list. Location will be important for many job-hunters – some need to be near elderly parents, some would like to travel, some want to stay in the area in which they were brought up, some can't leave it soon enough. Of course salary is important; for some, it's the most important factor, and most people need to earn at least enough to match their outgoings. Hours of work and holiday entitlement can be decisive in the choice. Some people, for example academics and medics, choose a job because they want to work with a particular person they respect professionally.

When you choose what job you want, you are (either consciously or unconsciously) putting a list of criteria like these into an order of priority and then checking each job against the list. The ones with the highest 'scores' will be the jobs you look at first and will want most. Of course the job does not exist that will satisfy every single criterion one has, but a job that satisfies the major criteria almost always turns out in retrospect to have been the 'right' one.

We carry out a similar evaluation in most decisions we make. They might be relatively minor choices, like whether we should holiday in Brighton or Barbados. They might involve the really big choices in life: What kind of person do we want to marry? Shall we want to start a family? Do we invite an elderly relative to live with us, or do we find a residential home for him or her? Do we want our children to be educated by the state, by private schools – or maybe at home?

I want to suggest that this is exactly how we should approach the business of voting, for I believe that Jesus, who constantly evaluated priorities and pursued a clear agenda of his own, would vote in the same way.

But how do we decide what our voting priorities are? How do we compile the checklist?

Christian Values, Christian Principles

In fact a number of Christian politicians and writers on political matters, over a long period of time, have compiled lists of criteria. They have identified essential strands in biblical thinking about the state, and have used them to discuss politics from a Christian perspective. Sometimes they make lists of 'Christian values'. The *New Shorter Oxford Dictionary* defines 'values' as,

> The principles or moral standards of a person or social group; the generally accepted or personally held judgement of what is valuable and important in life.

The seven cardinal virtues – faith, hope, love, wisdom, justice, fortitude and temperance – are an example of a list of Christian values, though it might be difficult to translate them into a manifesto.

Others have compiled lists of principles, items of conviction that should be promoted and upheld if a society is ever going to be considered a Christian society. Care for the poor is such a principle, the right to own personal transport is not. That doesn't mean owning a car is a sin, it simply means that car ownership is not one of the hallmarks of a Christian society.

Principles can easily be made into policy. How do you ensure that your society upholds the principle of care for the poor? You pass laws protecting the rights of the poor and you make provision for the state to provide what they cannot provide for themselves.

The ideal checklists, I believe, are those that identify Christian principles and are informed by Christian values.

The Contribution of William Temple

An influential Christian who set out principles for social governance was William Temple, who became Archbishop of Canterbury in 1942. In that year his best-selling *Christianity and Social Order* was published by Penguin Books. Temple was also a contributor, with other church leaders, to a Statement of Principles, drawn up to guide a post-war settlement, and is often regarded as one of the fathers of the Welfare State.

Temple believed that Church and State should keep within their own spheres of expertise. The Church had neither the knowledge nor the mandate to draw up plans to build bridges across rivers, for example, and engineers did not have the knowledge or the mandate to carry out the functions of the priesthood. On the other hand, if the government built a bridge that was dangerous and people's lives were at risk as a result, the Church had every right to condemn the state and its engineers. The Church, he considered, should guide the life of the nation, but should do so by broad principles rather than specific policy statements. It should condemn slipshod bridge-building, but it had no mandate to supply the government with a blueprint for a better bridge.

In *Christianity and Social Order*, Temple set out principles that he based on the Christian values he regarded as most important. He believed that this was not airy-fairy theorising but an intensely practical exercise. The values he worked with were these:

The family as the primary social unit

If politicians believed that the family was the most important basis for social order, he wrote, the quality of housing and leisure services would improve. People matter; families are not social statistics to be found somewhere to live. He also mentions the issue of Sunday trading, which is in our time, like his, an example of a debate in which Christians have played a major role, often arguing that Sunday trading is unfair to those who are not Christians, because it does not respect the right of the human individual to have a weekend for rest and restoration.

The sanctity of personality

William Temple believed that the right of people to organise their own lives and not be reduced to numbers and grey faceless units is a profoundly Christian value. He was writing about the same world that George Orwell portrayed in his novel *1984* (which was really about 1948). The sombre factory workforces, the implications of the new communist societies and the new fascism, and the dreary blighted landscape of post-war Britain all created a climate in which people often felt that they were just part of a machine. A Christian state, argued Temple, would make individuals feel significant.

There would be other social benefits: for example, better public health – 'an under-nourished and under-developed body is likely to house an irritable, querulous and defensive soul.'

The principle of fellowship

The third key value, fellowship, would promote educational values, believed Temple, by which 'the best things possible to men' might be realised: universal accessibility to education of all kinds, a fight against social snobbery, and a determination to end drudgery and insecurity in the workplace.

Archbishop William Temple was a theologian with an academic background in philosophy. But he wrote his book for the average man and woman in the street. He never suggested that his readers had to work out what the government's policies should be: that was the government's job. He did argue that Christians had a duty to set principles and values like these before the government, as targets toward which they could legitimately demand that government should aim.

So when he went on to set out 'Six Principles for Social Order' he was not writing a political manifesto. He was setting out what he felt people should have in mind as they scrutinised politics and politicians.

1. Every child should find itself a member of a family housed with decency and dignity.
2. Every child should have the opportunity of an education till years of maturity... This education should throughout be inspired by God and find its focus in worship.
3. Every citizen should be secure in possession of such income as will enable him to maintain a home and bring up children in such conditions as are described in (1.) above.
4. Every citizen should have a voice in the conduct of the business or industry which is carried on by means of his labour.

5. Every citizen should have sufficient daily leisure, with two days rest in seven and, if an employee, an annual holiday with pay.

6. Every citizen should have assured liberty in the forms of worship, of speech, of assembly, and of association for special purposes.

Of course you don't have to be a Christian to endorse most of the principles. Many political parties, and many religions, would gladly assent to them. But Temple was explicitly writing as a follower of Jesus. At the end of *Christianity and Social Order* he is careful to make that plain:

> This book is about Christianity and the Social Order, not about Evangelism. But I should give a false impression of my own convictions if I did not here add that there is no hope of establishing a more Christian social order except through the labour and sacrifice of those in whom the Spirit of Christ is active, and that the first necessity for progress is more and better Christians taking full responsibility as citizens for the political, social and economic system under which they and their fellows live.

So his contribution is extremely valuable in a discussion of the question, 'How would Jesus vote?'

The Tradition of Christian Democracy

William Temple was discussing social order at a time when the tradition of Christian Democracy was re-awakening in Europe.

Although Christian Democracy does not have a monopoly in Christian politics – all the major political parties have significant numbers of Christians as members, and there is a large Christian group in Parliament – it is an interesting example of a political movement that has its roots in

Christianity and in several parts of the world has campaigned on explicitly Christian values. I want to briefly look at its history here, though a full account would take a much bigger book than this.

Some historians argue that Christian Democracy dates from the days of the Emperor Constantine, very early in the history of the church. They say this because Christians from the beginning provided support and welfare for the disadvantaged and vulnerable – a task that is at the heart of historic Christian Democracy. Once, during a famine, Constantine even decided that the bishops, instead of the public official, should take over the task of distributing corn to the starving population. It's because of such episodes, and the extensive welfare programmes that the church has sponsored through the centuries, that some authorities claim that Christian Democracy goes back almost to the time of Jesus.[14]

That is rather over-stating the case (looking after the needy is a task Jesus commands all Christians to do). But concern for human and civil rights, economic and social justice and strengthening family and community continued to be a theme in European Christian thought until the theme was given a name by Pope Leo XIII, who was head of the Roman Catholic church from 1878 to 1903. He issued Papal Encyclical Letters that examined a range of social issues from a Christian viewpoint, and in one, *Graves de communi* (1901) he described Christian Democracy as organised action for the well-being of the people, 'to comfort and uplift the lower classes'.

Leo did not want the movement to become a political party, but in the troubled climate of late-nineteenth-century Europe it was probably inevitable it would. By the time the *Catholic Encyclopaedia* was published in 1908, the author of the article on 'Christian Democracy' was forced to concede regretfully that:

> The term Christian Democracy seems to have been seriously compromised by the action of those who distorted its meaning from that laid down in the Encyclical 'Graves de communi'. It therefore inclines to lose the meaning of 'popular Catholic action', and tends more and more to denote a school and a political party.[15]

Christian Democracy also arose as a political force outside the Roman Catholic Church. Indeed, the first Christian Democratic party to be founded in Europe was Abraham Kuyper's Anti-Revolutionary Party, a party of Protestant Calvinist inspiration (Kuyper, 1837-1920, perceived the French Revolution as a primarily atheistic uprising). After World War II, new European parties arose, anxious to continue the fight against dictatorship and to promote the cause of democracy. They included several new and revived Christian Democratic movements: for example in Italy there were the Christian Democrats, in Germany the Christian Democratic Union, in Holland the Dutch People's Movement, and in France the Popular Republican Movement. Some owed their inspiration to earlier Roman Catholic movements, others were Reformed in their outlook. Christian Democracy – 'politics without ideology'[16] – was reacting to the prevailing Marxist ideology and also to Liberalism which emphasised the freedom of the individual and made religion a private matter: Christian Democracy, by contrast, sees Christian values as making a difference to politics.

In the second half of the twentieth century the movement lost some of the strength it had immediately after the war but in several European countries such as Italy,

Germany and Belgium, Christian Democrats prospered and were sometimes in government. Their membership included several of the most prominent politicians of the time.

Christian Democracy also appeared in South America, originally as small breakaway parties inspired by Roman Catholic social teachings. In Venezuela, El Salvador and Chile the Christian Democrats became the governing party. In a continent dominated by what America perceived as a Marxist threat, Christian Democrats struggled against left-wing guerrillas in El Salvador during the 1980s and in Chile they embarked on major reforms. They were given substantial support by the United States who saw them as a bulwark against the kind of Marxist revolution that had happened in Cuba, but they were eventually defeated at the polls by Salvador Allende, who launched the Marxist initiative that the Americans had feared.

Christian Democracy has put down roots in a number of other parts of the world. For example in 1989 the Christian Democratic Union of Russia was formed – a tiny group of activists whose membership grew rapidly. Struggling against restrictions that made campaigning extremely difficult, competing with a host of new opposition parties formed since the revolutions of 1989–90, and also encountering harassment and obstacles from the KGB, by 1990 the party had four members on the Moscow City Council and one member of the Russian Parliament.

Britain and Social Democracy

Britain has no history of Christian Democracy comparable to that of the European countries. There are three main reasons.

First is the fact that Britain retained its Christian heritage for much longer than the European countries – there was no equivalent to the seismic shift represented by the French Revolution nor to the social upheaval of the 1848 revolutions, against which the nineteenth-century Christian Democrats stood. Atheism was not the socially disruptive force in Britain that it was in Europe, and political parties did not constitute themselves according to whether they were in favour of the religious status quo or whether they wanted to destroy it and replace it with something different. It is striking how many Christian Democrat movements outside Britain are parties of resistance or revolution – for example in Chile and in Russia.

Second, Britain is a Protestant country by constitution, and therefore does not have the links of Catholic history and church structure that the Catholic European countries do. Ideas spread very easily around Europe in a way that is much more difficult between an island and the continental mainland, and the Roman Catholic Church's communication structures by which information and news travelled around the continent were impressive even in mediaeval times. Also, there is no body of authority in Britain comparable to the papacy, and no way of disseminating information that has the authority and power to influence that Leo XIII possessed simply by being a pope.[17]

Third, Britain has for centuries been proud of her island status; even today, having been a member of the Common Market for decades, Britain has the reputation of being the difficult member, the one who makes a fuss, the one who doesn't quite fit in; and British politics are dominated by the question of whether or not we stay in Europe. A situation like that is hardly a good seed-bed to grow a historically European-inspired movement!

Detachment and Opportunity

In fact, the situation of Britain has been an asset rather than a handicap in the development of British Christian Democracy.

It makes it possible for the development of a truly home-grown Christian Democratic movement without the need to adapt to neighbouring movements or to be influenced by a particular, continent-wide way of doing things. It makes it possible for British Christian Democrats to respect the achievements of their European colleagues and the pioneers of the past, while at the same time drawing on the strengths of a tradition to which they do not have to conform in detail.

And that is what has happened. The Movement for Christian Democracy (MCD), which was launched in London in 1990, is both part of European Christian Democracy and separate from it. The major difference is that it is not a political party but an all-party non-denominational Christian group.

The core of MCD philosophy, enshrined in the founding 'Westminster Declaration' of 17 November 1990, is the 'Six Principles'. We will be looking at these in detail in the next chapter, but it's worth noticing here that they draw on earlier British Christian thinking rather than on European Christian Democracy *per se*, though again, the European influence is noticeable.

Thus British Christian Democracy had at its launch the best of both worlds. It could utilise and develop the best of British Christian traditions and perspectives, but it was also free to acknowledge that Christian Democracy has a particularly continental past.

So what does British Christian Democracy look like? And what are its Six Principles? We explore those questions in the next chapter.

Notes

13. Jimmy Carter, *Keeping Faith: Memoirs of a President* (Collins, 1982).

14. See, for example, the article by U. Benigni, 'Christian Democracy', in: *The Catholic Encyclopaedia, Vol. IV* (Robert Appleton, 1908).

15. *Ibid.*

16. Roger Scrutton, 'Christian Democracy and the Czech Republic' *The New Presence,* (Internet publication), August 1998.

17. This of course accounts only for the lack of a history of Catholic-inspired UK Christian Democratic parties. The lack of British equivalents to the vigorous Continental Protestant Christian Democratic traditions may, suggests my colleague Professor Prabhu Guptara, be due in part to the British class system.

3
Six Ways of Looking
at a Manifesto

The Contribution of the Movement for Christian Democracy

The Movement for Christian Democracy is not a political party. It is an all-party non-denominational Christian group, active at all levels of the political process and intended to combat the 'sidelining of basic Christian values'. The Westminster Declaration lists 'six guiding principles which highlight some basic themes of Christian Democracy'. They are:

- ❏ *Social justice* (as founded in the character of God and given by divine law)
- ❏ *Respect for life* (human beings are created in the image of God)
- ❏ *Reconciliation* (the kingdom of God is heralded by a community in which we are all to be reconciled in Jesus Christ)
- ❏ *Active compassion* (the God of justice is the God of love; we are called to active loving service of others)
- ❏ *Wise stewardship* (all economic activity involves our responsibility before God for the world entrusted to us)

❑ *Empowerment* (authority is given from God for the common good; those who have power are to be accountable)

It's interesting to put the Six Principles proposed by Archbishop Temple side-by-side with the six 'Guiding Principles' outlined in the Westminster Declaration, the launch document of the Movement for Christian Democracy.[18] One of the founders of the movement, Lord Alton, discusses Temple with admiration in one of his own books,[19] and Temple's thinking is clearly part of the movement's heritage.

The Declaration unpacks each of the Principles more fully. It is interesting to see similarities with a number of other formulations; interesting, too, that the Declaration announces the MCD's intention not to promote a political manifesto, but to make Christian values and principles part of the political process. Temple believed Christianity should be written into Government social policy; the Movement for Christian Democracy seeks to make this happen, by making Christian morality and perceptions a factor in political decisions. They do so by lobbying, discussing, interrogating candidates, and arguing the case in other ways.

It could be said that the MCD, because it is a pressure group and not a political party, is better placed to raise the issue of the values of Jesus. Some candidates have campaigned in the past as 'Christian party' candidates only to find themselves marginalized by the major parties. The big parties all assured the electorate that they endorsed the same values, so rather than vote for the (usually inexperienced) Christian candidate, wouldn't it be a much better use of the vote to support *them*, the tried-and-proven? A good many candidates have lost their deposits as a result of arguments of that kind.

The Emergence of Christian Political Parties

When my colleague David Porter wrote his *Back to Basics* (a study of public morality and ethical government) in 1994, David Campanale contributed the following paragraph to the discussion of the Movement for Christian Democracy:

> However, though the Movement itself would not become a political party, a party could well emerge from it. The Movement does not say it has the only Christian answer or approach to a particular issue: it would only claim, 'We are trying to marry biblical exegesis and principles with policy.' Scripture does not change, but policy develops. But in what political tradition would it grow? It would attempt to develop the best of British Christian roots and perspectives, but would acknowledge that Christian Democracy has a particularly continental past. In that sense the Movement is attempting to import a foreign ideal to Britain, but to make it relevant to the domestic situation. The Movement for Christian Democracy is free to (and does) choose or reject from the European tradition. It is not growing in a vacuum, but is confined by the traditions and principles of European Christian Democracy.

An example of a political party that has developed from the Movement for Christian Democracy is the Christian Peoples Alliance (CPA), which was launched in 1999. It has adopted the six principles of the MCD as its basis, and they are a central part of its manifestos. In the next six chapters, I want to look at each of these principles in turn.

Notes

18. Movement for Christian Democracy, 'The Westminster Declaration' (7-page A4 mimeograph, 17 November 1990).

19. David Alton, *Faith in Britain* (Hodder & Stoughton, 1991), pp. 18–19.

3.1
Social Justice

You've seen the TV documentaries, I'm sure. Crowded financial dealing rooms with long lines of video screens; young men and women staring intently at flickering rows of figures scrolling down the screen. Or the Stock Exchange trading floor, frantic bids and counter-bids, shouted over the background roar of immense sums of money changing hands. World clocks, prominently displayed, show the time in New York, in Tokyo, in Hong Kong, in Geneva. Backwards and forwards, over cables deep in the ground and far below the ocean, or bounced from earth to satellite and back again, inconceivable amounts of money are hurtling round the globe at speeds you can hardly dream of.

The City of London is one of the great financial centres of the world. From the legendary 'Square Mile', trillions of pounds cross the globe each day. Fortunes are made and lost, economies are strengthened and weakened, and the fate of millions of workers is decided.

Take the Commercial Road eastward out of the City, and after four miles you come to the London Borough of Newham. Three hundred years ago the area was a luxury retreat for wealthy Londoners. Today Newham is struggling. The area began to decline before the Second World

War and war damage, evacuation and emigration to newer suburbs only hastened the decay. In July 1994, Newham's MP, Stephen Timms, told the House of Commons,

> In Newham, we suffer from poverty and the effects of inequality to a severe degree. The Department of the Environment's local conditions index, which was published earlier this year, placed Newham as the local authority area suffering from the highest urban deprivation... the problems of poverty are closely linked with high unemployment... household incomes in Newham are considerably lower than for the capital as a whole... the borough had 9,000 over-crowded households – twice the London average. What do the Government think about inequalities and poverty on that scale?

Inequality there certainly is, and it's not just inequality of assets. There is also unequal access to resources. A City of London foreign exchange dealer once said to me, 'I can move tens of millions of pounds across the globe in seconds! But getting a thousand pounds in aid across to the borough next door, well, that's a different matter.'

From my own experience in business I know what he was talking about. When I was with Inlaks, for example, I had to move $2 million to New York. It was the 30 December and the money had to arrive by New Year's Eve. The bank had made an error and hadn't carried out my written instructions. I realised I had less than twenty-four hours to transact the deal; and I managed to do it.

But another time I had to send money to Brazil, funding for a homelessness project. The money went to the United States, where a cut was taken; then it went through another agency, who took their cut; then another, and so on. By the time the money reached Brazil it had shrunk to much less than I had sent, and it had taken a matter of weeks to arrive. An extreme case? Perhaps, but I traced the transaction all the way back, recalled the original amount and sent the funds directly to the project in São Paulo.

No wonder people often comment to me about the lightning speed of cash transfers in international business, and the tortuous path that charitable funding is often forced to take. There are layers and layers of bureaucracy and a host of other complications. Politicians have been very slow to take action.

Take the London Borough of Hackney, which is even closer to the City than Newham is. In Hackney, which spends more money on street cleaning than any other council, rubbish is rotting in the streets. Local services are closing down at a moment's notice, yet 17,000 housing benefit claims are, as we write, lying unprocessed in Hackney. A catalogue of disasters recorded in the *Economist* of 18 November 2000 – making Stephen Timm's report of Newham's problems six years earlier seem almost mild by comparison – included the bald statement that 'children's services are woeful'.[20]

It seems to me that when we challenge candidates and also government and opposition parties according to the principle of social justice, we need to ask them: 'What are your policies for boroughs that suffer higher levels of deprivation than others? And how exactly do you plan to make it happen? What do you see as the most effective way of bringing social justice to Hackney and Newham? How do you propose to reduce the difficulties of access to resources that Britain's poorest boroughs experience?' – and you could ask similar questions in many parts of modern Britain.

Thirteen of the twenty-five poorest boroughs in Britain

are to be found in London, and they co-exist side by side with some of the wealthiest boroughs. That statistic demands a response. It demands recognition of the inequality. It demands that a clear statement should be made: 'This is intolerable'. We need to demand the same of political candidates.

We need also to ask candidates what their proposals are for economic regeneration. For example, what are their views on the Information Technology revolution and its implications? IT can redress social injustice in a number of ways, but to benefit from that, we need policies of 'skill-ing'. We need training and education to help individuals to get employment, jobs and businesses into those British boroughs that are being ignored because they are getting poorer and poorer. It seems that more and more investment is directed towards those who are already doing well; the poorer boroughs are too often ignored. Social justice means that the opposite should happen. Specific, targeted help in the form of new business, work places and housing, should be brought into those boroughs, to bring about economic regeneration. The CPA promoted a London Regeneration Fund for the deprived boroughs. There is room for many similar initiatives.

Sound Business

You don't only have to appeal to politicians' better nature. You don't have to argue on moral grounds alone. The ethical necessity for social justice isn't the only argument that carries weight. You can urge politicians to promote social justice on the grounds that social justice is a very sound business proposition.

Re-skilling and providing resources to people in disadvantaged boroughs will result in an explosion of microbusiness enterprises. For example, information technology can be used to regenerate business, provided that we put our minds and hearts into it. An executive of one of the largest software out-sourcing companies in Britain told me that in London alone, there are 100,000 IT job vacancies. Yet the level of unemployment in some London boroughs is as high as 25%.

It hasn't gone un-noticed. A company on whose Board I serve, for example, made a proposition to the Government, as a contribution to the New Deal project. We would provide very simple recruitment tests that could be carried out in the deprived areas. The tests would ignore colour and age, and evaluate people purely on merit and aptitude, to identify which candidates had an aptitude for a career in IT. Those candidates would immediately be given jobs and training opportunities.

I'm talking about London because that is the area in which I have practical experience of these matters. But the challenges are nation-wide. All around Britain there are communities that are dying – economically, socially and spiritually. As the situation worsens, social problems increase. It is said by some social observers that disadvantaged communities tend to have higher crime rates, because residents of those communities see crime as the only way to obtain vital resources like food and clothing.[21] Most British cities have seen community life deteriorate in their most disadvantaged districts, in pace with economic decline. Unemployment, for example, is not just a personal catastrophe that wrecks family Christmases and makes family holidays impossible. Unemployment means very low levels of disposable income. That in turn means less maintenance of dwellings – faced with the choice of mending the gutters or buying food and clothing, the decision is not hard to make. The consequence is housing decay, and declining local amenities.

As I write, I have just been told the very sad story of a Ugandan Asian family living in London. In December 2000 their Local Authority issued them with rail tickets to Southend (about sixty miles away, and at least an hour's journey by road), and told them to be out of their accommodation within twenty-four hours: they had been rehoused in Southend. The accommodation in question was housing into which they had moved when they arrived in Britain in 1972. There was a reason for the enforced move, of course. The property had deteriorated to the point where it was judged unfit for occupation and was condemned. But what a way to deal with people! Their jobs were nowhere near Southend, and one of the family was undergoing hospital treatment at the time. How could anybody deal with such extreme challenges?

Although it is often talked of as a moral problem, social justice is at heart an economic problem; few of the key issues can be dealt with without cash injections. That is why I am excited by the London Regeneration Fund I mentioned earlier; it makes interest-free loans, removing the burden of debt servicing from those who need a financial helping hand. On a bigger scale still are schemes like the Employment Bond scheme that has been launched by the Jubilee Centre under the directorship of Michael Schluter. It's essentially a rolling capital funding scheme. Currently being developed in Newcastle and Sheffield (and with a research group considering an East London Employment Bond), the scheme calls for capital from businesses and individuals on an interest-free basis for a period of five years. You can do a lot with a capital sum in five years, even if you have to give it back at the end! The interest that the money earns over five years is used to generate either business capital to create workplaces, or homes. It's a creative way of addressing the social justice agenda. It's also interesting that the East London Employment Bond is being launched because of the success in Sheffield and Newcastle. London is not always the place that invents things first, by any means!

Michael Schluter points out that the Employment Bond scheme is not just about economic regeneration. It is also about personal and spiritual regeneration.

> Unemployment causes not just hardship but bitterness. The unemployed often feel no one really cares. Employment Bonds are a way of demonstrating that local people do care and these Employment Bonds are also a way of starting to create trust and goodwill across cultural barriers that divide our cities.[22]

Rhetoric and Practice

Have you heard the one about the Minister whose advisors were trying to make him understand a proposed new departmental initiative? 'I can see how it would work in practice,' he said, 'but I just don't see it working in theory…'

Political parties and candidates are very good at making broad sweeping statements, and are especially good at talking theoretically. They readily agree that Britain has massive problems and that something must certainly be done about them. You will not find many candidates who will disagree with you, if you say that politics is as much about creating social justice as it is about anything else.

But we must ask our candidates more.

As we think about the way Jesus might have cast his vote and how he would have scrutinised manifestos, it's helpful, I think, to go back to the portrait we have of Jesus in the Gospels. As we saw in Chapter 1, he was a master of the unexpected question. Faced with an obviously disabled man his question was not, 'Would you like me to heal you?' but 'What do you want me to do for you?' The question was designed to expose the real problem, not the one that appeared superficially to be the whole of the man's plight.

What we need to carefully consider is not whether the candidate realises the problems. Most candidates wouldn't be allowed on to the hustings if they didn't realise the problems. The question is what solutions they think will work. Hard, practical policies are needed, not just talk, and there must be a prospect of delivery.

It's not a pipe dream; many projects exist, for example the work of the Social Investment Task Force, and its welcome proposal for tax incentives for businesses in deprived boroughs. This initiative will be a valuable incentive for corporate and private investors in Employment Bond schemes.

I have been privileged to be involved in projects that have addressed such issues. I was co-chair, for example, of a scheme run by Race for Opportunity London, Project Full-Employ, and the London Research Centre. We succeeded in obtaining half a million pounds from the Government Office for London with the following mandate: to create, in partnership with private enterprise, a thousand jobs. We didn't make that target, but we created several hundred jobs. They were jobs that hadn't existed before, and the project was a learning experience that can be built on, fine-tuned and sharpened to create even better results next time.

Notes

20. 'Will the government intervene to clean up the mess in Hackney?', *The Economist*, 18 November 2000, p. 43.

21. I would agree that there is some correlation between poverty and crime, but I am reluctant to generalise about the matter because it's all too easy to create stereotypes. At worst, it is possible to create a situation where disadvan-

taged communities – such as black people, poor people and unemployed people – are automatically assumed to be guilty of crime just because they *are* disadvantaged.

22. From personal conversation with Ram Gidoomal, December 2000.

3.2
Respect for Life

The second principle might be described as the natural out-working of social justice into justice for the person. It is described in the Preamble to the CPA Constitution in the following words:

> We believe that government must uphold, respect, protect and defend all human life as given by God and made in the image of God. We will work to ensure that each person, from conception to natural death, irrespective of religion, economic status, ability, attribute, colour, gender, race or ethnicity is given entitlement to equal respect and dignity.

The principle of respect for life is one of the most difficult issues. The real-world decision-making that it calls for almost always involves cases where there is personal anguish and deep pain. It's easy to theorise about abortion in the safety of a seminar room or a debating society. In the real-life situation, where several lives – not least that of the unborn child – are in trauma, emotion and rhetoric often run high. Nevertheless the principle of respect for life is one we can't back away from as we evaluate political agendas.

Christians and other religious people have traditionally had a great deal to say, understandably, on these matters. For example, Cardinal Thomas Winning, head of the

Roman Catholic Church in Scotland, has frequently spoken out on what are often called 'pro-life' issues. Sometimes the Cardinal urges a proper pace of debate, as in his intervention in the human cloning debate in late 2000:

> The Cardinal said the proposed 14-day limit for experimentation, after which it could not take place, was arbitrary. He also voiced 'alarm' that MPs would spend just 90 minutes debating the issue before 'crossing the moral Rubicon' and voting on it. 'Ninety minutes. No more. No longer than a football match,' he said. (*The Times*, 27 November 2000).

Pro-life values and the Issue of Abortion

Cardinal Winning has also made practical proposals aimed at defusing situations in which the only options seemed to be choices between two extreme positions. In a much-publicised case in Scotland where a twelve-year-old girl became pregnant, he said that he would personally pay the child to keep the baby rather than allow her to be forced to abort it. Many people interpreted this as extreme fundamentalism running rampant, but it was actually a moderate proposal. It was an attempt to avoid the extreme solution of abortion and allow a whole range of choices to come into play. After the birth, for example, a number of alternatives would exist for that baby's upbringing and for where and with whom it could live. If the birth happened, the various options could be considered. On the other hand, terminating the pregnancy would take away all the choices except one.

One possibility that has increasingly been explored in recent years is the provision of counselling centres, paid for by local authorities and made available throughout the country so that women can have a choice about their pregnancy. One of the cruel ironies of the abortion debate is that the phrase 'pro-choice' is usually hi-jacked by those who would like to reduce choice by claiming that the only choice is to abort. Many who take Jesus' respect for life seriously would like to broaden the range of choices. The foundations for such a service already exist in the centres of counselling and support that have been established across Britain, largely funded by donations and small grants, such as the 'Life Houses' run by CARE and LIFE, in which pregnant women can stay during their pregnancy.

Such initiatives should be built upon. The conviction that respect for life is not just a philosophical tenet, but is something that requires practical outworking, has led groups like the CPA to call for local authority funding, both for telephone helplines and local premises. Such funding would recognise and work with facilities already in existence and people already doing the job. The chief role of local and national government, in fact, would not be to provide buildings and money (though that would be part of it), but to build networks of support and co-operation between centres, so that the whole system is strengthened. Existing centres, too, could help local communities and organisations concerned about increasing the choices available, to bid for funds to set up centres of their own. Properly handled, such initiatives would not be a cost to society but an investment in its future.

Euthanasia

In late 2000 it was announced that Holland had become the first country in the world to legalise 'mercy killing'. This came as no surprise to those who knew that, for many years, the Dutch government had turned a blind eye to 'assisted death' which numerous Dutch doctors had offered for years. Yet it was widely felt that a step had been taken that would be difficult to reverse and which led into uncharted territory. The Vatican condemned the new law, saying that it 'violates the dignity of the human person'.[23]

The case for euthanasia, or allowing the right to die at a time of one's own choosing, has always been a profoundly difficult topic. Most people have known somebody, often a close relative, who has contracted a terminal disease or a wasting disease that humanly speaking offers no hope of recovery. Knowing the inevitable deterioration as the disease takes hold, and the terrible way in which victims of such conditions frequently become unrecognisable as the people they once were, patients and relatives have longed for some way in which the patient can face death with dignity while still in possession of a clear mind and the ability to take some control of his or her own affairs.

Expressed in those terms the case for euthanasia deserves respect even if one profoundly disagrees with it; after all, not many of us have to deal intimately with the issues for ourselves.

The issue of whether it is right to demand that a patient struggle on in terrible pain rather than end it all immediately has been transformed in recent years by the advances that have taken place in pain control. Pain management is now a major element of terminal care. But the euthanasia debate ranges much more widely than death as an alternative to a painful life. 'Mercy killing' at the request of a dying individual is not the only aspect of this difficult subject. The challenges become acute when the decision on what constitutes a liveable life – a life *worth* living – is made by outsiders. Abortion and euthanasia share some of the same challenges, as the stress on those who look after the dying relative or the disabled child enters the equation.

Christians and members of many other faiths would want to question whether a life that is apparently pointless really does have no point. Who is to say that a disabled baby with every prospect (humanly speaking) of a life with nothing but pain and frustration, won't when older claim that his or her life is as rich and full as anybody else's? We simply cannot play God in this way. We don't know enough.

Magdalena Kewerich, an eighteenth-century German woman, was afflicted with very poor health. She finally died of consumption at the age of forty – one of her son's earliest known letters is a cry of grief over her death. She had suffered several miscarriages and had contracted venereal disease. Health is just one of several problems she struggled with; social conditions, family history and her age also made pregnancy a perilous experience both for her and for the child.

So when she became pregnant again, the prospect must have seemed grim. If she had gone to a doctor to discuss the pregnancy, he would certainly have urged her to have an abortion. His concern might well have been as much for the child as the mother. The foetus would most likely be undernourished and was very likely to be born sickly. Several of Magdalena's children had died in infancy. What sort of a life would the child have, if it survived? Surely the life of such an individual would be so limited that it wouldn't be worth living.

The fact that makes this story stand out is that Magdalena Kewerich was the much-loved mother of the great composer Ludwig van Beethoven. Had she taken a doctor's advice and terminated the pregnancy, she would have aborted one of the greatest composers in history. Though her motives would have been understandable, she would have been cutting off at the outset a life that by any standards must be considered a valuable and meaningful one.

A large number of disabled people have argued the same case, eloquently and vigorously. Some, like Nabil Shaban the actor, have become distinguished in their chosen careers. Others, like the members of the Independent Living movement, have confounded the experts by leaving residential care and living in their own homes, the cost of attendant care being far less than the cost per person in a residential centre.

Somebody facing the onset of a debilitating and destructive disease might feel that life will shortly have nothing to offer and that a dignified assisted death is the best way forward. But it is fortunate for humanity that Professor Stephen Hawking thought otherwise. This brilliant scientist who has been compared to Isaac Newton and Albert Einstein suffers from ALS, a form of motor neurone disease that has robbed him of speech and mobility:

> Up to 1974, I was able to feed myself, and get in and out of bed. Jane managed to help me, and bring up the children, without outside help. However, things were getting more difficult, so we took to having one of my research students living with us. In return for free accommodation, and a lot of my attention, they helped me get up and go to bed. In 1980, we changed to a system of community and private nurses, who came in for an hour or two in the morning and evening. This lasted until I caught pneumonia in 1985. I had to have a tracheostomy operation. After this, I had to have 24 hour nursing care. This was made possible by grants from several foundations…
>
> I have had motor neurone disease for practically all my adult life. Yet it has not prevented me from having a very attractive family, and being successful in my work. This is thanks to the help I have received from Jane, my children, and a large number of other people and organisations. I have

been lucky, that my condition has progressed more slowly than is often the case. But it shows that one need not lose hope.[24]

The argument for terminating apparently unproductive and pointless lives is often made by people who argue the case on grounds of compassion and with great concern for those afflicted. If there is nothing left to life more than a vegetative existence, with no prospect of recovery and only the bleak prospect of further deterioration and perhaps pain, isn't the most compassionate help that one can give, the opportunity of an early escape?

One has to respect the integrity with which many people have come to this point. But it's also inescapable that we simply do not know enough about prolonged illness and vegetative states to make an absolute ruling. There are well-documented examples of people who were diagnosed as incurable who have made a partial or full recovery. And this is not a matter of miraculous cures (which most Christians would agree are quite possible) but of the pathology of the disease itself. It's a very large step, therefore, to legislate on the basis that prognoses are always correct.

We do not know a great deal, either, about long-term coma and related conditions. In hospices for the incurably ill, staff are trained to avoid discussing apparently comatose patients when they are within earshot. They know that the patients might be able to hear every word. There have been cases where the patient recovered from the coma and said that they understood much more while in that condition than people had assumed. And if a patient is capable of rational thought and of following a discussion about his or her own future, it's surely the most extreme cruelty to decide their fate without attempting to ascertain their wishes.

It's a veritable minefield and few situations fit into neat

categories. But there are biblical criteria that are helpful, and which have been adopted by Christians campaigning in these areas: for example, the CPA manifesto affirms that 'hospitals and residential homes will be asked to look at their policies towards the treatment of the elderly... It is never justified to treat elderly people as less entitled to life and respect merely because of their age or because of frailty.'

Respect for life, whether it be the life of the defenceless foetus in the womb (said to be the most dangerous environment any human being will ever be in, because of the statistics regarding abortion), or at the frail and vulnerable twilight of life as old age advances, or at those points in between where the value of a life through illness or other setbacks is often held to be reduced, is a vital principle for the politics of any caring society.

But it's much more than a philosophical and ethical banner under which to march. This is a costly principle; it comes with a price attached. Does the candidate or party that seems to be committed to a pro-life stance understand the consequences? Has adequate provision been made to deal with those consequences?

It means that hospitals, residential homes and indeed any institution which has an impact, or an influence on the elderly, will have to initiate policies for the treatment of the elderly that respects them and acknowledges that they have as much right to life as anybody else.

It means making practical provision for the increased number of single-parent families that will be created by a fall in the number of abortions. Does the pro-life candidate who is looking for your vote have a policy for helping them with housing, help with looking after the baby, and ideally some kind of training so that, if she wishes, the mother can go on to a satisfying and fulfilling life and career when the child is of school age?

It means that if euthanasia remains illegal there will be more old (and some younger) people alive who are going to need care in long-term illness, disability, or frailty. The Government will have to pick up the tab for that as well. Has the candidate made provision for it in his financial promises?

Bringing 'Jesus principles' into the task of voting is more than flag-waving. It can increase the burden of care. But no society can be called compassionate if it neglects to protect its weakest members. The weak and vulnerable were a high priority for Jesus, who would certainly have them in mind were he deciding whether or not to endorse a particular political programme.

Add to this the fact that respect for life is often an unpopular position to hold. I will never forget the experience of a debate in the 2000 London Mayoral election hustings at St Paul's Cathedral, where both Ken Livingstone and the Green Party candidate received louder applause for their pro-abortion, pro-euthanasia and gay rights stance than I received for promoting a perspective shared with me by people from all faith communities. And to think that this event was organised by the London churches! It was also the largest gathering during the Mayoral campaign. Over 2,000 people attended.

But Jesus, who was used to preaching unpopular sermons, spoke of the care God bestows on the sparrow. If God cares for such a tiny life, how much more does he care for the lives of human beings! And if we want to be like Jesus in our voting, respect for life is something we must care about as we scrutinise manifestos and promises.

Notes

23. 'Vatican Fury at Euthanasia Vote', *Catholic Pictorial*, 3 December 2000, p. 1.

24. From Stephen Hawking's website.

3.3
Reconciliation

At the heart of the Christian gospel is reconciliation. In fact the gospel is reconciliation: its claim is that Jesus Christ died on the cross, God as man, reconciling the world to himself, and rose again. It's a sobering reflection on all human disagreement and tensions that they take place in the perspective of a cross that represents absolute reconciliation. Followers of Jesus have a stake in seeing human beings reconciled to each other, because they themselves have been reconciled to God.

So how does that work out in practice?

Let me give an example. It's a story that I tell very often. I'd come from Geneva to Scotland to tour the factories that the Inlaks Group, my employers, had acquired. I stepped out of the plane into a clear Scottish afternoon. It was my first visit as Managing Director of Highland Seafood. Soon I was being driven through the lush countryside of Aberdeenshire in a comfortable car. The Production Director – a tall, rather dour man – pointed out local landmarks. Suddenly there the first factory was: tucked away in an attractive estuary, a curl of smoke from the salmon-smoking plant lazily ascending into the blue sky, and a car-park where we came to a halt in a section satisfyingly labelled 'Managing Director'.

We went inside. A number of key staff had been assembled to formally greet me – a kind of welcoming committee. They looked nervous and tense, as well they might. Two hundred people knew that the change of ownership meant they were about to lose their jobs. They didn't know that we planned to re-employ them immediately. I began to shake hands, moving down the line.

Something peculiar was happening as I greeted my new Aberdeen workforce. The bristling suspicion that had greeted me as I walked in was evaporating. When I was introduced to each staff member as the new Managing Director, barely-suppressed hostility turned to welcoming smiles. I would have thought that my job title would have identified me as one of the enemy, but here I was being warmly welcomed.

I wondered about it for a while, and even more so when the same thing happened at the next factory: initial hostility, disappearing when my new colleagues discovered that I was the new Managing Director they had been told was due to arrive. Several months later I asked the Production Director to explain what had been going on. He hesitated for a moment, then smiled.

'To be absolutely frank, Ram, we all thought we were getting an Englishman... '

It's the same kind of xenophobia that underlies the football slogan I've sometimes heard in Scotland: 'We support Scotland and any team that is playing against England'!

'There's this Irishman...'

I tell the story because in fact the major conflicts between human beings are in a sense easy to understand – and, in principle, easy to deal with. Usually conflicts nearer to home are more difficult to sort out. And we need to ask our political representatives, and those who want to become our political representatives, what plans they have made to deal with the invisible tensions that need reconciling. How do they propose to demolish the stereotypes that successive governments have (often by default) endorsed? The answers to these questions are at least as important as their prepared statements on foreign policy and international relations. Does it matter to them that many Asians in Bradford feel despised by the majority population? That the children of the unemployed are often ostracised at school, by children whose parents are more fortunate?

Stereotypes are a curse of modern life; they define social alienation. In Northern Ireland, religious labels that have, for a large part of the community, long lost their religious meanings, now divide the region. It's true in Kenya, where I have spoken to Christian congregations that found it immensely difficult to abandon the learned distrust between African, Asian and European communities. It has in the past led, for example, to the mass expulsion of Asians that brought my family to the UK. It was humbling and exciting for me to be invited back by the Church of the Province of Kenya to help them build bridges between Asians and Africans.

In Eastern Europe, ethnic divisions can mean that Christians living in the same street never talk to each other, let alone pray with each other.

And in Switzerland I remember once being asked by a hospital registrar what religion I was, and telling him that I was a Christian: he shook his head. 'The computer's only got Protestant or Catholic for that,' he said.

Many stories like those are told as jokes today – we're all familiar with Irish jokes, and in continental Europe they have Polish jokes and others too. But the jokes are not really very funny. They emphasise division and difference, and mock diversity that should be celebrated. They actually make a much deeper point about the desperate need for reconciliation. Of course devolution has solved some problems, but in the long term ethnic divisions remain. Devolution satisfies the agendas of several ethnic groups, but it also creates distances between other communities. And any political manifesto, if it is going to make a serious attempt to heal the wounds that modern society displays, must address the matter of reconciliation.

So one of the big questions we must ask political candidates is what their plans are for achieving a political framework that respects differences, yet treats everyone equally and has reconciliation at the heart of policy proposals. I think that's part of achieving the principles of Christian Democracy; celebrating and respecting differences but not allowing those differences to increase the distance between communities.

Of course there is room for humour as we enjoy the differences between the various communities that make up Britain today. But there is always a danger that at worst it will cross the bridge into racism, and at best it will become a gentlemanly way of implying perceived superiority and inferiority that has no basis in fact and certainly no place on a Christian agenda.

My Neighbour the Asylum Seeker

That's why I am enthusiastic about an initiative of Home Office Minister Barbara Roche that she calls the Refugee Integration Strategy. It aims to look at those applying for entry into the UK, not as people to be given handouts and treated as second-class citizens, but as individuals with their own aptitudes and abilities, and often qualified in their home countries in areas in which Britain is very short of skills. I've been part of an initiative called the Employability

Forum, which has a mission and mandate to help those who have come off the asylum seekers list and are now free to work in this country. But they are still waiting for the results of their residency application, which means that many employers won't consider them because their future is uncertain. Add to that the fact that Britain still has a lot of racism in society and in its institutions, and these people begin to look as if they are caught in a limbo, neither in nor out.

I believe that corporate business needs to be made aware that there is a pool of people to draw on when recruiting. For example, Britain is facing a huge shortage of trained doctors. But among the refugees arriving in Britain are those who are qualified doctors in their own countries. So one initiative that is now being explored is to fast-track recognition of the qualifications of the doctors and nurses in this category, and bring them into our health services.

This is reconciliation. It brings together communities that were once alienated. In fact it carries out the biblical mandate on the treatment of aliens: their dignity and worth are to be recognised, and their displaced status is not to be a reason for regarding them either as a threat or an inferior species. The book of Ruth is a beautiful example of God's requirement for the treatment of aliens. How does your local political candidate measure up to that? You might, for example, ask him or her for their opinion of initiatives like the ones I have just described.

Reconciliation is supremely 'vertical' – most of all, in the grace of God shown to humanity on the cross. But it is also 'horizontal'. Reconciliation is needed between God and human beings, but also between human beings and human beings. One way of achieving this is to bring people together on common ground with a common cause. Let me illustrate from my own Indian background. In the Indian sub-continent there is deep division between Indians and Pakistanis, going back certainly as far as 1947 and Partition. In the UK it is often different. You would not often find in the subcontinent what I find very often in Britain – Indians and Pakistanis sitting on the same committees, two expatriate communities on neutral ground in which a measure of reconciliation is possible and a resolution of tensions that existed back in the sub-continent.

So when I and a group of colleagues set up a charity primarily working with South Asians, we called it the South Asian Development Partnership – not the Indian Development Partnership or the Pakistani Development Partnership. The name is a step of reconciliation. It recognises a community of people who share common ancestry and ethnicity in the broad sense of the term: language and a heritage of traditions. We want to take advantage of what is held in common and build on that, rather than focus on differences that will only divide and cause division and more distance and more separation.

Reconciliation at this level is being promoted in many ways. The Eastern European Forum is a similar bringing together of Slavs, Latvians and a range of other peoples on neutral ground to build understanding. And of course the United States is a good example of how, despite a multitude of ethnic problems, much has been achieved in recent years to bring together separated groups in networks and forums sponsored by federal and state authorities.

The effect of this kind of practical reconciliation is not only that local relationships improve and a productive reconciliation begins, but also the effects of reconciliation sometimes feed back into the communities' countries of origin – and all the more powerfully because the message being sent back is usually in the context of economic muscle.

3.4
Active Compassion

You will probably have seen the wonderful 'Peanuts' cartoons by the American humorist Charles M. Schultz featuring a group of children whose social circle includes a dog, Snoopy. One of his cartoons is a mini-textbook on the subject of active compassion. Charlie Brown and Linus are walking through falling snow, wrapped up warm in overcoats and woolly hats. They see Snoopy, sitting alone in the snow and shivering. 'Snoopy looks kind of cold, doesn't he?' comments Linus. 'I'll say he does,' replies Charlie Brown, 'maybe we'd better go over, and comfort him.' They go over. 'Be of good cheer, Snoopy,' says Charlie Brown. 'Yes, be of good cheer,' says Linus. They walk off. Snoopy, still shivering, watches them go, a perplexed question mark hovering over his head.

It's easy to be compassionate if all you have to do is say compassionate words. Words, the old proverb says, cost nothing. Schultz, himself a follower of Jesus, makes the point well. People are averse to costly compassion. When I was campaigning in the London Mayoral elections, a journalist said to me, 'You want a transport policy that caters for disabled people? That's going to be very expensive.' My immediate response was to ask him what place compassion has in politics at all, if there is no place for compassion towards our most needy citizens?

But the journalist was also blind to the fact that there are sound business reasons for compassion. If people won't be convinced by an appeal to their sense of compassion and social justice then let them consider the business implications of compassion, just as we touched on the business advantages of social justice earlier. Consider slavery, for example. People were taken away from their villages in Africa. Families and whole communities were destroyed. When anti-slavery campaigners like Wilberforce argued that slavery must be abolished, he was appealing to social justice and to compassion: whole industries and entire economies were dependent on one set of human beings being subservient to another, and exploiting that situation to create wealth. Slavery was an offence against every one of the six principles we are discussing in this section. It violated respect for life, it violated social justice, it disempowered its victims. And the driving force behind Wilberforce and his fellow-campaigners was compassion for people who had been abused.

But there is another side to the equation. People said that abolishing slavery would lead to the break-up of Western economies and the destruction of Western communities (something that they saw no problem in subjecting others to). They prophesied business losses running into what in today's terms would amount to trillions of pounds. The result, of course, was nothing like that, and new business networks and trading relationships emerged that would not have been possible in the days of slavery.

As I write, the good news has just been announced by Chancellor Gordon Brown, in early December 2000, that Britain is to write off millions of pounds of Third World debt. It is the culmination of much campaigning by organisations like Jubilee 2000 (whose name reflects the fact that writing off debts owed by the poor to the rich is a good biblical principle!), and publicity by major media figures such as Bono of the rock group U2. But although the case for compassion was immensely strong in itself (Britain spends more per annum on chocolate than the entire GNP of some of the countries involved), there will be business benefits as well. Active compassion is not only more effective than mere words, it also creates a climate of mutual benefit: biblically, casting one's bread on the waters means that your bread returns to you in due course (Ecclesiastes 11:1).

Releasing Potential

So for me compassion is something that we must practise because we are told to practise it and it is to be practised for its own sake. Yet my experience is that when you act in compassion towards a particular sector or group, the group that is benefited finds, in an amazing way, that its potential is released. Actually, it forces you continually to examine your own motives: Did I really act out of compassion, purely and simply? Or was there a business agenda, conscious or unconscious, behind my actions?

I believe that we must examine all political programmes with this aspect in mind. Compassion, if it is to deserve the name – whatever the underlying formula, equation or interpretation might be (and some of the secondary business benefits help the original recipient of the compassion as much as the giver) – must spring in the first place from a genuine desire to help those who need help, who ask for help, who cry for it, who deserve it.

That's why I challenged the journalist, who wanted to talk to me about transport policy, on two levels. His comment (and he was a Christian journalist, which made his comment all the more shocking to me) that catering for disability would be a very costly policy prompted my immediate reaction: 'Where is compassion in society? Are you saying we can't afford it as a society? If you are saying that, look at the wealth locked up in the Stock Exchange and the Treasury, and in Western economies generally. However we choose to argue the point, that wealth is there, and the differential continues to exist between the haves and the have-nots.'

Of course it was appropriate to go on to the second level. 'Apart from that, look at the sheer business case. A transport policy that serves disabled as well as able-bodied people would release numerous people to travel to jobs that would otherwise be unreachable. So we'd be addressing the skills shortage by maximising the mobility of the whole population to get to areas of need. More than that we would be constructively addressing the dependency culture. Too often in the past the only choice we have given certain sectors of society is dependence or nothing. But this policy is one that literally mobilises, that creates community out of sectors that have previously been marginalized and made to feel hopeless and useless.'

I had to make the point because he had not seen it for himself, and in a world that is often driven by self-interest and profitability, such arguments can be powerful persuaders. It is a side-effect with real benefits.

But that is not why we should exercise active compassion. We should do so because it is right and proper to do so. It is something that we should consider if we want to reflect on how Jesus would vote, because this principle of Christian Democracy is inspired by the teachings of the churches, and hence ultimately by Christ himself, who taught that we should love our neighbours as ourselves, that we should love the poor, and that we should take care of those who don't have what they need (Matthew 22:39).

Disinterested Compassion

One of the astonishing developments in charitable initiatives of recent years is the explosion of mass giving through events such as Bob Geldof's Band Aid, which began the trend. A large number of rock musicians joined forces to produce a record and a live concert that raised millions for global aid. Today, mass charitable projects range from Comic Relief to TV marathons like Children in Need.

Events like these are mixed blessings. There can be no doubt that they have raised awareness of global needs and have given charitable work a high profile in popular culture. The work of a project like Comic Relief, in particular, has been immensely valuable in many ways: comedians are not always rich, and some who have given time and money to work for Comic Relief have done so at considerable personal cost. The methods of fundraising used are intelligent, the money donated is effectively monitored and long-term commitments made. And it's especially helpful that Comic Relief, mainly through some inspired film documentaries, has avoided the visual clichés of newsworthy poverty – pot-bellied starving children who appear more as symbols of poverty than as portraits of real people – and instead showed that the people they help are kids and adults just like us and our neighbours.

On the other hand, big charity splurges tend to create the illusion that charity is a fun, occasional activity, a chance for communal mayhem and the warming knowledge that money is being raised for needy causes. They are less effective at teaching the public that compassion is costly and can't be picked up and put down like a tennis racquet, to be employed every now and then.

In the context of government, there has been considerable concern expressed that these events – particularly the TV 'telethons' – take the responsibility of care away from government and in effect make the public pay for what should already have been covered by taxation. And some groups, like the disabled community, have criticised the telethons for what they consider to be a patronising attitude to caring for the disabled; why should disability services have to be funded by one-off jamborees in which bank managers tackle stupid dares and schoolteachers put on silly hats?

I have not had much involvement with telethons and mass-media events, and though I can understand and sympathise with many of the objections, perhaps charity that is wheedled out of people is better than no charity at all. It's certainly an area where much thought needs to be invested in evaluating political programmes. But one question that should be asked, I believe, is this: does the political candidate or party that you are evaluating regard charity and acts of public compassion as add-ons, to be exercised at intervals with a great deal of fanfare and publicity – or as a continuous thing, a part of citizenship as important as education or care of the elderly? And should it be paid for out of the public purse to which all contribute, or out of the proceeds of occasional festivities?

In my own work in the charitable sector I have seen young people in Britain who were mobilised to raise funds for people within the developing countries. It wasn't patronising, and it had no trace of colonial arrogance. We established criteria as to where funds that were raised should be sent. They were to go to the nationals of the countries concerned. Our criteria for projects was that they should be national-driven, holistically conceived and with a good track record. We said this because we firmly and passionately believe that the nationals of the country know and understand their problems best – and that it is therefore best to exercise compassion and prove them capable. Compassion exercised in that way liberates and unites communities.

But we need look no further than our own country to find many examples of situations where active compassion could, and should, be a liberating and uniting force. In my own city, London, we have wild variations between the efficiency of housing lists and success in tackling health inequalities. It simply cannot be right that life expectancy for men living in Bromley (a south London borough) should be four years longer than it is for men living in Lambeth (a poorer area).

There is much to do at home. But compassion should be global. I am a Patron of the Emmanuel Hospital Association in India. The Association builds hospitals that treat a range of diseases and disabilities which without hospitals would be fatal. During the Kosovan war, doctors from the Association went out to Kosovo to help treat casualties, a project which we organised with the help and backing of Muslims, Hindus and several other religious groups.

Sometimes we become too accustomed to statistics. The shocking discrepancy across Europe in mortality and disease statistics, for example, is too easily filed away and forgotten. It was brought sharply to my mind when a colleague mentioned that a Hungarian friend had recently moved from Hungary to a new post in America: one of the most compelling reasons for his move was that in America his children could expect to live fifteen years longer than they could expect to in Hungary. There is a great deal of opportunity to get involved in changing people's lives, and you don't even need to go as far as India to do it.

Social Justice and Active Compassion

As we close our discussion of active compassion it may be useful to make a distinction between compassion and social justice – for the overlap between the two is one of the underlying reasons for charity sometimes becoming patronising.

I would suggest that justice is to do with the restoration of rights, and that compassion has to do with the giving of rights. Take, for example, the example of refugees. When I arrived in Britain in 1967, an Indian from East Africa twice displaced from my homeland, I did not regard myself as having rights. Few refugees do: what they are looking for are solutions to their immediate crises, of housing, food, clothing and money to live on.

True, I was a member of a Commonwealth state, but I was aware that I was entering a country where I had paid nothing into the system. I'd never paid taxes in Britain: what right had I to benefit from the public purse? What right had I to demand to be educated?

I had a passport, but it didn't make me British. It was endorsed 'British protected', so I had no automatic right of entry. I had to queue up with others in a line marked 'Aliens'. I was granted entry into the UK by the Immigration Officer, who used his discretion. His decision, benefiting one who had no rights, was therefore an act of compassion.

Today's refugees and asylum seekers are in a similar situation. On the day this is being written I have been alerted to the case of a man of Middle-Eastern origin who has had to change his identity. He is not able to open up the past and cannot return to his home country. His life and work are spoken of as having been marked by integrity and resourcefulness. He is an engineer and a qualified pilot. Yet our systems, institutions and procedures militate against such resourceful people easily finding employment here.

An asylum seeker has no right to employment until his papers are approved – after which he usually has the right, but nobody wants him. At that point social justice and compassion are intertwined, but active compassion is the essential starting point.

Another, similar example is the ex-offender, newly released from prison. In one sense he has no rights. His situation is part of the punishment for a crime he committed. In another sense he does have rights, because he has discharged his debt to society, served his term of imprisonment and should now have the rights of a citizen again. But the overwhelming majority of ex-offenders find that the only way forward is if somebody shows them active compassion.

That gives us another angle from which to evaluate political programmes. Governments often pride themselves on their record of social justice. But if social justice and active compassion are as closely linked as they seem to be, there is good reason to challenge governments on their record of compassion. Sometimes politicians who seem to score highly on the scales of justice make a much less impressive showing when it comes to compassion. Jesus, who destroyed the distinction between master and slave and gave dignity and worth to the marginalized and excluded of the society of his day, would surely insist that both are of immense importance.

We need to look for compassion that is not chequebook compassion, that doesn't think money will solve every problem. But as we said at the outset, active compassion is costly; we may not be called to do much with our chequebooks, but we will almost certainly be called to do a lot with our diaries.

Chequebook compassion is limited to those with money. But I have been amazed at the range of people who are engaged in active compassion – disabled people, for example, confounding the common belief that you can't do active compassion unless you are able-bodied. Actually, it's across the board. All of us can and must be involved. One of the most exciting charitable ventures I was ever involved in is Christmas Cracker, which I founded with Steve Chalke. The initiative that garnered most publicity was our Christmas Cracker Restaurant project which raised thousands of pounds for relief work and gave young people experience in entrepreneurism and a taste of running a small business. It was a project run by teenagers (and was very empowering for an age group that has not always been considered mature enough for management responsibility). But I and my family visited one of the restaurants and were very moved to be served by a disabled lady in her eighties who was really thrilled to be involved in the project.

Can teenagers really do anything useful? Of course they can. Aren't old people past the age when they can help in active compassion? Of course they aren't. Across age, across gender, across income bracket, across ethnicity, the call is to active compassion in the fullest sense of the term.

3.5
Stewardship of Resources

We live in a shrinking world, and we are exploiting resources in a reckless and selfish way.

The prosperous North eats four-fifths of the world's annual production of protein, two-thirds of the world's annual grain supply, and seven-eighths of the world's annual production of petrol and gas.

The prosperous North contains one-quarter of the world's population.[25]

The question 'How would Jesus vote on issues affecting the environment and natural resources?' is not immediately easy to answer. There are not many environmental issues in the Bible. It's rather like asking whether Jesus would have read a daily newspaper. But there is no doubt that Jesus would have an opinion on environmental matters and the squandering of resources. The right treatment of the planet matters to him – because he created the planet. It's his handiwork.

> In the beginning was the Word, and the Word was with God, and the Word was God. He was with God in the beginning. Through him all things were made; without him nothing was made that has been made. (John 1:1–3)

So Jesus takes the natural interest a Creator takes in his creation. But he also takes a critical interest in what humanity is doing with the world in which we live. Genesis 2:15 describes mankind being given a responsibility to look after the environment that has been created for him: 'The Lord God took the man and put him in the Garden of Eden to work it and take care of it.' The responsibility is a large one. As more and more demands are made upon the environment, and precious natural resources are opened up to serve the needs of technology and a growing global population, the choices become critical. The desolation of the rain forests and the scarring of landscapes by open-cast mining are fairly easy matters upon which to form an opinion. But what about the balancing of the need for housing and the need to preserve a viable rural economy? Or the need to create industrial resources, while preserving an unpolluted and enjoyable environment? Decisions like that demand careful thought, if we are seeking to discern how Jesus would vote.

The Changing Planet

Thinking of that order was on the agenda in November 2000 when the Eco-Summit was held at the Hague in Holland. It was to be an opportunity for delegate states to get to grips with world ecological issues and chart a way forward: their aim, no less than the saving of the planet. But I heard one cynical comment at the time from a member of the public: 'Look who's coming to the Hague! Lots of Americans! And who controls the American agenda? Businesses, not government.'

He was right. America is controlled by big business; the role of government is in many ways being sidelined. For example, the US Government discovers that there is a popular demand for reduction of dangerous industrial emissions from 50% to 30%. But business uses its financial muscle to lower the figure to 5% – and that is a statement of intent, rather than an explicit commitment. Globally, businesses are negotiating the Green agenda, buying out their targets and negotiating targets downwards. Commitments once regarded as binding are being watered down into wishy-washy statements of intent, down to what is manageable and expedient. New technology seeks to exploit new resources, and the cost of preserving the environment in the process of extracting those resources is often considered to be an operating expense not worth paying. Modern business makes huge demands on the environment, but those who make the decisions are rarely those who suffer the consequences.

But the eco-system itself demands drastic measures. The world is changing. The year 2000, the first year of a new millennium, was notable for natural disasters such as the floods in Britain – the worst for centuries – and the prolonged and heavy rainstorms that produced them. Elsewhere vast holes were developing in the polar icecap, matching gaps in the ozone layer, and climatic change was widespread. Almost all commentators pointed out that such catastrophes had been prophesied for a long time. Many pundits had warned that the effects of commercial exploitation of the environment would come home to roost sooner rather than later.[26]

Government's role is changing. Control and power are, in real terms, passing into the hands of the big corporations. My colleague Professor Prabhu Guptara has pointed out that the trend is for more and more businesses to merge, merge and merge again until you get a dozen or so megacorporations that are global. You don't have to dream up a conspiracy theory to explain it. It's in the nature of business, as new technology and widening markets demolish the boundaries and border tariffs of the past. They control everything, and the whole issue of democracy is side-lined. Is one person really worth one vote any more, if that vote is technically impotent?

I know that there is concern in some quarters and that some multinationals such as Shell have programmes to repair the damage that their business causes. But they are in a minority. There is tacit consent that most of the rain forests, the coral reefs, the British Green Belt and many other, previously 'safe' environments, will have to be sacrificed to the needs of the new millennium and its people.

The Green Movement

One reaction to the threat to environmental resources is the Green movement, which is a widespread grass-roots response and involves many more people than vote Green in elections. It includes various strands. There is a *mystical strand* that sees the earth as a mother to be protected and revered: this strand is part of the modern rise of neo-pagan-ism.[27] There is what one might call a *science-fiction strand* that sees a threat of a gleaming world of the future, in which synthetic resources will be the norm because natural resources will all have been used up. Among Christians, some hold to a *prophetic evolutionary view*, which reveals a faulty view of creation[28] and sometimes is as bad for the planet as is the most greedy secular commerce. And there is the concept of *stewardship* – which I believe is how God describes human responsibility for natural resources in the Bible.

The Green Party in Britain has made considerable progress, as it has done in Europe. But other parties too have a stance on the matter – or should have, for their policies almost always use up resources. So when we are evaluating any candidate or party one of the questions must be: What is your view of the stewardship of resources? And how much confidence do you have that you will have the opportunity, if elected, to put your view into practice?

The relationship between government and business in this respect is a very complex one, and is today being increasingly talked about. For example, in October 1999 I was one of three speakers delivering a Hansen-Wessner Memorial Lecture in Oxford.[29] The lecture theme was 'The Role of the Business Corporation as a Moral Community'. I spoke there of:

❏ The need to help developing countries with their debt payments – another example of the responsibility to achieve social justice

❏ The global implications of environmental issues, *e.g.* the ozone layer, and also the problem of polluting the Danube as it traverses Europe.

[These points] illustrate a developing view of company law away from a duty merely to maximise shareholder value, to that of a duty to balance the triple bottom line: monetary value, environmental impact and social justice.

In this broader sense, the stewardship of resources is very relevant.

The best way to help somebody is not always to feed him or her directly. That's the point of the much-quoted slogan, 'Give a man a fish and you feed him for a day: teach him how to catch fish and you feed him for a lifetime.' One project in which I was involved – a Christmas Cracker beneficiary – was a scheme to plant trees in Ethiopia. I will never forget the applications that came in for the trees. We made it a very public, transparent scheme because we wanted to make a point. Some of our supporters said that we should be giving food and water, that we should be loading up trucks with emergency supplies and sending them out to Africa. One reason we didn't do that is that others were doing it already: Bob Geldof and Band Aid, for example, were sending much-needed supplies to the starving people out there. But the main reason is that we saw the tree planting as extremely relevant in the rebuilding of Ethiopia. The famine was caused by a combination of political greed by the countries rulers and a failure of the natural ecology. Planting trees was a major step towards repairing the ruined natural resources of Ethiopia. So we were anxious to develop the stewardship of resources in that global context.

Accountability

We have seen that Jesus' view of the natural world is the proprietary view of the maker and also the critical view of one who is assessing the performance of those he has left in stewardship of the natural world.

There is a third way in which Jesus views the way humanity deals with natural resources. Exploitation and development of the environment, of the order that makes substantial changes to it, are always initiated by the rich and the poor have no voice or power to object. The wealthy nations believe that they need even more, and the extra has to come from somewhere. All those second cars and environmentally damaging luxuries do not come out of an inexhaustible pot of resources. The US State of Texas – with a population one-third that of Britain – emits 20% more greenhouse gasses than does Britain.[30] Where do the necessary resources come from to repair what is spoiled? The more we take, the less there is left for others.

So Jesus also views our use of resources as a matter of social justice. Who suffers by our use of resources? And what are we doing to put matters right?

A good example is the damming of rivers to create power and water supplies, usually with catastrophic results for the local environment. In India, the novelist Arundhati Roy is opposing the building of a dam, leading local opposition by villagers who will be made homeless and impoverished by a development over which they have not been consulted.

In Eastern Europe a dam on the Danube between Hungary and the Czech Republic has altered the natural environment and destroyed a wetland in Hungary – which in turn has had a major impact on the local economy.

We have already mentioned the problem of some European countries polluting the Danube as it passes through their territory. It's a trans-national issue. Britain has a poor record in the matter of 'acid rain' – atmospheric contamination from British industry has caused blight in Scandinavian countries. Nearer to home still, in the London Mayoral elections I was not the only candidate to campaign with a manifesto that included strong measures to reduce London's traffic pollution.

The Role of Government

All the issues we have discussed come back to what the role of Government should be, taking into account the fact that in some national and global contexts the buying power of large corporations diminishes the powers of government wholly to act as they might wish.

One way of evaluating politicians' attitude to the stewardship of resources is to look at what they propose to do to create partnership between government, business and citizens. For example, I believe that companies developing IT and other low-pollution, high-intensity/low-space consumption industries should be rewarded by tax and rate concessions, if only as a start-up benefit. I believe that people affected by developments that they cannot control and which dramatically reduce their access to, and enjoyment of, natural resources should be compensated much more sensibly than the existing compulsory purchase and other payment levels. I believe, too, that people should be encouraged to switch resources, so that dependence on diminishing and usually polluting fossil fuels would be replaced by cleaner and more plentiful fuels. Cyclists should be given every encouragement, by a system of excellent cycle routes throughout our major cities (Vienna, a pioneer in this, would be a very good model to imitate).

We have spoken, too, of natural resources, but other resources should be made widely available. The benefits of computer, IT and internet resources should be available for everybody – and that means overhauling the present creaky UK telephone infrastructure. There should be facilities for training people in their thirties, forties and fifties (and older) in technologies that can seem bewilderingly complex but which their children and grandchildren operate without thinking.

How would Jesus vote on these issues? I believe issues like the ones we have discussed would be high on his agenda. I am sure, too, that he would not treat this matter in isolation, any more than he would do so with any of the Six Principles.

In the end, the theology of natural resources is inextricable from the theology of their Creator. Tim Cooper, a member of the Green Party and a Christian, puts it like this:

> Green theology may be defined as being centred upon God as revealed in Jesus Christ and concerned with the structure and function of the whole creation. It should offer a new understanding of human 'dominion' over other creatures, encourage a growing appreciation of the intrinsic goodness of creation and seek to understand the true scope of redemption. Theologian Jürgen Moltmann writes of the need for a doctrine of creation which is 'directed towards the liberation of men and women, peace with nature, and the redemption of the community of human beings and nature from negative powers, and from the forces of death....' Christians should recognise that by misusing the Earth we are showing contempt for our Creator. It is precious to Him; it *matters*.[31]

The fact that large numbers of Jesus' followers have not only ignored the destruction of resources but have also sometimes collaborated in their destruction is a tragedy. It's also a rebuke and a challenge to Christians today. Jesus more than once rebuked his very religious hearers that non-believers sometimes listened to God better than believers did: for example,

> This is a wicked generation. It asks for a miraculous sign, but none will be given it except the sign of Jonah. For as Jonah was a sign to the Ninevites, so also will the Son of Man be to this generation. The Queen of the South will rise at the judgment with the men of this generation and condemn them; for she came from the ends of the earth to listen to Solomon's wisdom, and now one greater than Solomon is here. The men of Nineveh will stand up at the judgment with this generation and condemn it; for they repented at the

preaching of Jonah, and now one greater than Jonah is here. (Luke 11:29–32)

And it's sobering to read the anger of a modern neo-pagan, contemplating the abuse that the twentieth century inflicted on the natural world:

> I think the time is coming now when we have to take the responsibility by the throat and actually get out there and say, 'There are answers here: I'm not prepared as a pagan, as a priest, and as a practising witch to sit back and see my planet, my mother, raped any longer.'[32]

If Jesus' followers had really listened to him and treated the world they live in differently; if they had raised their voices when others abused that world, and cried out against greed and exploitation that placed the majority of the world's resources in the hands of a favoured few – then maybe people like that would have had less to be angry about.

Notes

25. Figures compiled by Christian Aid, quoted by Kathy Keay, *How to Make the World Less Hungry* (IVP, 1990), p. 78.

26. In fairness it should be said that some experts are not convinced that human mismanagement of resources is the reason for the current spate of natural disasters. But at the very least, it's a factor – as you will find if, for example, you visit flood-devastated towns in Britain and ask the residents whether they think that Government has learned enough lessons from the past to protect their properties now.

27. A good discussion of this topic is in David Burnett, *Dawning of the Pagan Moon* (MARC/Monarch, 1991).

28. This point is well developed in Albert M. Wolters, *Creation Regained: Biblical Basics for a Reformational Worldview* (1985: Paternoster Press, 1996).

29. The lectures are sponsored by the ServiceMaster Foundation and the Said Business School, Oxford, and funded by the ServiceMaster Corporation – an American company founded on Christian business principles.

30. Today, BBC Radio 4, 18 December 2000.

31. Tim Cooper, *Green Christianity* (Hodder Spire, 1990), pp. 267, 270.

32. Nigel, a Wiccan high priest and contributor to *Hallowe'en: Trick or Treat?* (Video, Jeremiah Films).

3.6
Empowerment

I have a friend and colleague called Sam Pitroda. Sam has a passion for providing telephones for under-developed countries. He talks about telephones with a visionary enthusiasm. He leads his company WorldTel with the fervour of a moral crusade. Telephones may seem an unlikely topic to get passionate about, but then we Westerners tend to take them for granted. WorldTel's brochure delights in statistics, like the fact that there are more telephones in the city of Tokyo than there are in Africa.

But what's so special about telephones?

Yellow Telephones

Telephones, explains Sam, mean empowerment. He illustrates by telling his own story. He left his home in Orissa, India, as a young man and went to America to study electronics and find a job. Within a few years he had registered over fifty telecommunications patents; the industry was a latter-day gold rush and Sam was in at the beginning. He became a dollar millionaire three times over, and today the innovations he patented are still being used all over the world.

Now seriously rich, Sam couldn't forget the poverty he had left behind in India. He had a strong sense of obligation; he wanted to share his good fortune with his mother country and introduce the new technologies that were changing the world. Eventually he persuaded the Gandhi government to endorse his dream of putting a telephone in every Indian village by the year 2000. He went back to India and led an enthusiastic team of brilliant young Indian engineers, all of whom could have gone to America and become wealthy. But they wanted to work with Sam. The team broke all the rules, defied all the conventions, confounded all the pessimists and finished the job. Sam's salary as director was one rupee (less than two pence) per annum.

Today you can see Sam's yellow telephones all over India. They mean that impoverished Indians living in remote villages aren't powerless any more. Now they have connectivity to a much larger network. They can telephone their MP, they can have a presence in a much larger space; previously they were imprisoned in their isolation, now they have a small foothold in places where decisions are made that affect their livelihoods and their families.

And they now have the power to be involved in their own welfare. They can order goods and services from nearby cities. They can ring to ask for medicine to be put on tomorrow's truck, instead of waiting for a truck to arrive that happened to have the medicine they needed on it.

Of course it's an empowerment that is only a beginning. Will the MP want to talk to the villager who wants to talk to him? What if the desperately needed medicine costs three months' wages?

Sam readily agrees: empowerment is not just a matter of telephones, but of social change. But the yellow telephones have transformed many Indian lives. Many disabled people, for example, have jobs operating village telephone exchanges. Before, they would have been beggars.

The Largest Church in Europe

Did you know that the largest church in Europe is being built in Hackney, London?

Hackney is the London Borough I mentioned earlier (p. 63), the one with escalating social and environmental problems. It's also the place where the Kingsway International Christian Church (KICC) is situated. KICC's pastor, Matthew Ashimolowo, has a vision for a church that will seat 5,000 people. His present church building is a former warehouse that holds 4,000 – twice as many as Westminster Abbey and almost twice as many as the largest traditional church in London, St Paul's Cathedral. The congregation is so huge that large television screens have been erected to allow everybody to see the service.

Pastor Ashimolowo's large congregation is drawn from all over London. Many of the members come from much more prosperous boroughs than Hackney. If you were choosing the most prestigious location for Britain's biggest church, Hackney might be quite low on your list of options. At the time of writing the borough is £40,000,000 in debt and is technically bankrupt. Black people, who often feel powerless, feel even more powerless in Hackney.

I recently spoke at Pastor Ashimolowo's church. As I drove across London to Hackney I had a vision of KICC as a huge resource of black Christian leaders and black Christians. From such a people-resource might emerge people who could stand for election as local councillors, and have a say in the decisions that affect their community's life and fortunes. But who will have the political vision to bring the community into empowerment, to have a say in its own future, to propose its own solutions to the problems that the community understands best of all, because the community comprises the people who experience the problems?

Which candidate's manifesto has the vision for that kind of change?

Engaging in Politics

This is a very personal matter for me. Until I became actively engaged in political campaigning, I felt disempowered as a Christian. I didn't feel part of any system that could influence the running of my country, bring about change and make an impact. I felt that I was living at a distance from the decision-making process.

Then I became involved in the Christian Democratic movement in Britain and began to think hard about proportional representation and engaging in the political process, and I realised that it was possible for an individual to matter.

A single voice is always a small one, however. It was frustrating to talk to the major political parties about issues important to Christians. The big parties seem happy to take cheques from Christians but are not always so ready to listen to our concerns. That's not empowerment.

When I joined the Christian Peoples Alliance and began campaigning as their candidate for the London mayoral election of 2000, there were frustrations of a different kind. Now I met Christians who told me firmly, 'It's unbiblical to vote.' Often they believed that because their great-grandparents had believed it. The message had been handed down, generation to generation. A sixty-year-old man told me, 'I've never voted in my life. This is the first election in which I shall be voting. I'm making an exception because of you – but I still feel uncomfortable doing so.'

It was frustrating for me, because as a Christian candidate I naturally hoped that Christians would be a large sector of my supporters, and to be told that the whole exercise was founded on theological error was distinctly depressing! But I discovered that when you are able to show such people that the Bible does not say that one should not vote, that in itself is a form of empowerment. You are enabling people to have a say in the political process who previously, through their own misunderstanding, had no voice. I believe that kind of teaching is a task that some Christians should take up as a real commitment.

But there is another reason why some people don't vote, and it has nothing to do with beliefs about the biblical case for political involvement. While campaigning, I met a large number of black and Asian people who told me, 'I'm not even registered to vote. I don't know how to get involved in the system.' In those cases, the simple act of explaining how to register as a voter was an act of empowerment. More: being on the electoral register actually brings a great many other rights and opportunities. I was able to say to people, 'So you're on the register now. You know what that means? You can be candidates in local elections. You can run for a seat on the local council!'

That was the vision I had, driving to Hackney through filthy streets and depressed housing. A church congregation, if it really wanted to, could be a presence in local politics, elected and mandated to transform the borough. For example, black majority churches are ideally placed to respond to such challenges. In their congregations are many gifted people with the skills and temperament to be successful in local politics and possibly at national level too. In North Acton, for example, the Redeemed Christian Church of God (RCCG) has acquired a warehouse opposite the Underground station: externally it's an unremarkable building, but inside it has been transformed. High technology, attractive furnishings and striking interior design mean that entering the church is like entering a different world!

Active community churches that are already working to meet the social needs around them are ideally placed to engage politically with their local community. It is not out of the question that church members could even become the governing group on the council.

That might sound sinister, but it isn't. It is what empowerment means. If you have a badly-managed council and you are a registered voter, you have the basic qualification to ask your neighbours to vote for you as candidate for change. If you can persuade a number of other people to join you in your campaign, you are beginning a political movement, just as the first Greens did, the first Conservative, Labour and Liberal members did, even the first Raving Monster Loony Party members did.

It might also sound far-fetched. What has Jerusalem to do with Athens? What does a church know about running a large London borough? Go to Hackney and see how a church like the KICC has taken over old warehouses and refurbished them to the highest standards. The KICC is running services, events, activities, sub-groups. There is a large reservoir of organisational and planning brilliance. Imagine that being translated into the local council – even, in due course, to government. That simple act of empowering people could turn out to have an enormous impact on society.

It's a process that has already begun. One of the most interesting aspects of the black majority churches is that members of those churches have requested the CPA to set up a political awareness training programme for interested members. Several hundred people have signed up for it and receiving training in the whole political process and how to become engaged with it. A new urban guerrilla movement? Not at all. It's a programme to introduce people in the ethnic minorities to rights and opportunities that the rest of us take for granted.

I am a Trustee of the Institute for Citizenship. Our title says it all. Our remit is to teach citizenship, to a wide variety of people. As a Trustee my priority is to ensure that we help minority communities to understand what citizenship means, in its fullest sense. It means participating in society, making your vote count, having an impact. In that connection it's a great satisfaction to me that the Institute is working with the organisation Operation Black Vote; we are very impressed by the work they are doing, with limited resources, to mobilise the black community to vote.

It brings back to my mind the terrible time when the Asians were expelled from East Africa, when my family and thousands of others lost their homes and their property and were forced to seek a home overseas. One reason it happened, I believe, is that many Asians had been very reluctant to take up citizenship. Their fear was, 'Will we ever be accepted by the Africans?' – but that same unwillingness contributed to their eventual rejection by the African Community. Teaching citizenship and its practical outworking, in its fullest sense, is of the utmost importance if barriers of fear are to be broken and bridges of confidence built.

Running for Office

It was an amazing experience for me, as a member of one of Britain's ethnic minority communities, to join the Christian Peoples Alliance and later to become their candidate in the London mayoral election. One in three Londoners is from the ethnic minorities, yet I was the only party candidate who was black. The fact that a black candidate was standing was tremendously empowering, not only for me – I'd engaged with the system at last! – but also for local communities. Almost every day, even now, I still meet people from the ethnic minority communities and churches who say to me, 'It was so exciting to see one of us, somebody from a refugee background, running for one of the biggest offices in the country!' There was something tremendously empowering in that fact alone.

On the other hand it was extremely dis-empowering to realise that none of the main political parties in the London Assembly had put forward an Asian candidate. It was disempowering to find that in the Scottish and Welsh Assemblies, where PR exists, there is no Asian member; and in Scotland and Wales there are no ethnic minority members at all. That is a very serious disenfranchisement of a large people group.

I am not saying that only black people can represent black people. That's not the point. But I *am* saying that in what is widely held to be a fair, transparent, open system of democracy, it is very strange to find in the mainstream political arena not one ethnically-elected candidate, even on the PR list system, who has been given this opportunity in Scotland and Wales.

The Meaning of Empowerment

All sorts of political movements have claimed the word 'empowerment' for themselves. It has acquired meanings that embrace some of the most violent revolutionary aspirations in history. It was empowerment that Marx and Lenin demanded, and the results changed the world.

Perhaps the sense in which I have been talking about empowerment is less seismic, but it too can change the world.

The simple acts of getting people to register to vote, to iden-tify with the system so that they have a feeling of ownership of the political process, and spreading the vision that a very few people can make a huge impact, cannot but change the political landscape dramatically and permanently.

In the London elections the Christian Peoples Alliance, with less than a hundred members, secured, in a hundred-day campaign, more first preference votes than the Green Party and the UK Independence Party.[33] Both those parties were granted a free political party broadcast by the BBC, on the grounds that they had MEPs in the European Parliament. We were refused a broadcast. I asked for a meeting with Anne Sloman, Chief Political Advisor to the BBC, to ask why we had not been granted a broadcast too. She explained that we were ruled out because we could not prove a political following. It was intensely disempowering because we were already hearing from our campaigners that people were saying that if we had more visibility we would have attracted more votes. Across the capital, people were saying, 'Of course you didn't get a broadcast. You're not a mainstream party.'

But is that democracy? The number of candidates was small. The opportunity to make a political broadcast gave several of those candidates an advantage. British legislation includes measures to facilitate empowerment of all people groups, but media control of the means of promoting polit-ical manifestos made that impossible in the mayoral election.

Empowerment was a key factor in Jesus's ministry, whether it was a matter of giving a sector of society dignity and a voice in a way that it had not had them before (for example, his treatment of women), or releasing people from the bonds of disease or social stigma. It was, like all his concerns, intertwined with other issues. Empowerment is related to social justice, compassion and much else.

Empowerment, in spiritual and political terms, is a theme that runs through the Old Testament prophets, not least in Isaiah, of whose prophecy Jesus is the centrepiece. Jesus, who knew the Old Testament scriptures intimately and was fully aware of his own role in them, would have been taught the following passage from Isaiah 61 while still a child. It is a passage that represents a key strand in his political thinking, and it could stand as a foundational text not only for the principle of empowerment, but also for the whole Christian Democratic agenda.

> The Spirit of the Sovereign LORD is on me, because the LORD has anointed me to preach good news to the poor. He has sent me to bind up the broken-hearted, to proclaim freedom for the captives and release from darkness for the prisoners, to proclaim the year of the LORD's favour and the day of vengeance of our God, to comfort all who mourn, and provide for those who grieve in Zion – to bestow on them a crown of beauty instead of ashes, the oil of gladness instead of mourning, and a garment of praise instead of a spirit of despair. (Isaiah 61:1–3)

Note

33. The victory was a mathematical one. By one of the ironical quirks of proportional representation, I secured enough votes, as head of the CPA 'top-up' list, to take a seat on the Assembly, but a threshold, introduced to keep the British National Party from having a disproportionate representation in British politics, also kept me from taking the seat! In the vote for Mayor, the Greens received fewer first preference votes than the CPA but many more second preference votes.

4
Single-issue Politics

Everybody can remember what they were doing when they heard that Princess Diana had died. Images of her funeral have become part of the national collective memory. The flowers, the slow motorcade, moments from the Abbey service... There are many moments from history that stick in the mind like that. Happy times, like the demolition of the Berlin Wall. Sad times, like the assassination of J. F. Kennedy.

Tony Blair's landslide General Election victory in 1997 created a crop of images to add to the collection. Some of the most enduring were the television pictures of the victory of ex-BBC reporter Martin Bell, who had campaigned in Tatton against the sitting MP. Symbolically clad in a white suit, he stood as an independent candidate on an anti-sleaze ticket. He vowed that, having made his point, he would sit as Tatton's MP only for a single term.

In the run-up to the 2001 general election, he announced that he planned to stand as an independent again. The curious thing was not his decision to stand as an MP again, but his decision to fight the Conservative-held constituency of Brentwood and Ongar. He told reporters that he had been asked to stand by the local Tory Party, whose members claimed that the local association had been 'infiltrated by evangelical Christians'. As Conservative Central Office didn't want to intervene, local Tories had asked him to stand as an independent against the sitting MP Eric Pickles.

It would be rash (and premature) to attempt an analysis of what happened in Brentwood and Ongar in this book. The story is certainly a lot more complicated than early reports of Martin Bell's intentions suggested. It centred on the activities of Peniel Pentecostal Church in Brentwood. A year earlier the newspaper the *Essex Courier* had been making serious allegations. They claimed that Peniel had infiltrated – and now controlled – the Brentwood and Ongar Conservative Association. As the allegations contained serious attacks on the Trustees of the church (which is a member of the Evangelical Alliance), they took the paper to court and won a convincing victory. The *Essex Courier* was forced to withdraw all its allegations. The newspaper's lengthy front-page apology ended a campaign against the church in which comparisons had been made with cult fanaticism in Waco, Texas, and in Tokyo.

This is not the place to chronicle a story of which the repercussions are still rippling in the constituency. The reason I mention it is that it was considered newsworthy that Christians should be visibly involved in local politics. You don't find newspapers reporting that humanists have taken over a constituency or that a particular left-wing constituency has a majority of Marxists. But the news stories on 8 December 2000 didn't even draw attention to the stories of Waco-style megalomania, or of ultra-disciplinary brainwashing cult-style leaders, that had been made in the local press. For the media news programmes the term 'evangelical Christians' seemed to be enough to hang a story on, and to imply subtly that any responsible political party needs to be protected from influxes of such people.

Why should it be considered so remarkable that evangelical Christians should get into politics or have an influence in local affairs?

A Christian Mind – or Not

Sadly, it is largely the Christians' own fault.

For a large part of history, the Church has kept its distance from secular politics – and, indeed, from secular thinking itself. Of course there have been great exceptions, when individuals and sometimes entire churches have engaged with the secular world and turned it upside down. In this book already we have mentioned the work of William Wilberforce, who led a great revolt against slavery, one of the foundations of the western economy of his day; and the Confessing Church in wartime Germany, whose members like Martin Niemöller and Reinhold Niebuhr taught and practised defiance against the might of the Nazi regime. There are many people and groups of people who might just as well have been quoted, who believed that the church's role in the world was intended to be transformational as well as devotional. Mother Teresa of Calcutta put it memorably when she described the members of her Order, the Missionaries of Charity, as 'contemplatives living in the world':

> When there are no more poor, no more hungry, no more lepers – then we will retire to our convent and give ourselves entirely to prayer... But I hardly think that time will come...[34]

History is full of people like that.

But there have been many periods when the Christian voice has been almost silent in secular discussions and few people have been aware that Christians have a point of view on secular issues of the day. And that has usually meant that Christians have not been thinking in a Christian way; indeed, that there is no Christian mind being brought to bear on issues of the day. Pietism has often meant world-flight, and sometimes absurdly so.

Amy Carmichael, the great evangelical missionary to India, told of a dream that she had had. In her dream she saw a group of Christians sitting in a circle, near the edge of a precipitous cliff. A few hundred yards away a silent queue of people was slowly approaching the cliff-edge. One by one, they fell to their deaths. She approached the seated circle and saw that they were absorbed in making daisy-chains. She shook them and shouted at them to look at what was happening to the long line of people. 'Go and stop them!' she screamed. 'They're all going to die!'

'Oh, we couldn't do that,' one of them said to her regretfully. 'You see, God has called *us* to make these daisy-chains...'

The current climate of Christian involvement in the arts, in science, in politics, in the media and much more has its roots in the early 1960s. It was a period when Christians like C.S. Lewis were bringing rigorously thought-through biblical principles to bear on a wide range of issues, but most still lived in a world divided between sacred and secular without much traffic between the two. It was not that there was a lack of a presence in secular ideas, but that there was hardly any Christian *thinking*, because Christians had become used to thinking in secular ways and according to secular principles.

The literary critic and Christian apologist Harry Blamires expressed this powerfully in 1963 in a book that became a best-seller:

There is no longer a Christian mind.

It is a commonplace that the mind of modern man has become secularized. For instance, it has been deprived of any orientation towards the supernatural. Tragic as this fact is, it would not be so desperately tragic had the Christian mind held out against the secular drift. But unfortunately the Christian mind has succumbed to the secular drift with a degree of weakness and nervelessness unmatched in Christian history...

There is no longer a Christian mind. There is still, of course, a Christian ethic, a Christian practice, and a Christian spirituality. As a moral being, the modern Christian subscribes to a code other than that of the non-Christian... As a spiritual being, in prayer and meditation, he strives to cultivate a dimension of life unexplored by the non-Christian. But as a thinking being, the modern Christian has succumbed to secularisation... There is no Christian mind; there is no shared field of discourse in which we can move at ease as thinking Christians by trodden ways and past established landmarks.[35]

Blamires' book was a key element in a flowering of Christian engagement with secular culture, the fruits of which we are still seeing today. But he was not just talking about the situation in 1963. He was describing a mentality that recurs through history. And if Christians lose the concept of a Christian mind, and the secular world is unaware of what Christian thinking about politics looks like, is it any wonder that the sudden eruption of evangelicals into a local constituency party, for whatever reasons, is considered to be strange and probably sinister?

One common type of thinking in some Christian circles has been described as 'single-issue' thinking. It can be seen in some sectors of American evangelicalism but is also often to be seen in Britain and in Europe.

Single-issue politics could be compared to the process we discussed in the previous section, where six principles were proposed to act as yardsticks against which policies and programmes could be evaluated. The difference is that in single-issue politics, the list of principles is reduced to one.

In the Candidates' Forums that are organised by churches in many constituencies at election time, you can often see this kind of thinking. A candidate is asked a question that's clearly meant to find out where he or she stands on a particular issue. That issue is obviously the one issue that stands (in importance) above all the others as far as the questioner is concerned.

It might be abortion, or a similar pro-life issue. It might be something to do with religion in education. It might have to do with safeguarding the rights of believers. It may be a media issue, or the fight against pornography, or the dangers of the Internet. Whatever the question, you can tell by the questioner's reaction whether this is a single-issue situation or not. If it is, when the questioner receives the 'right' answer he or she will ask no more questions: the candidate has passed the crucial test. But if the answer is not the one that was wanted, the questioner loses interest in the candidate. His or her other views and policies are of no further interest.

There are two reasons why this is a problem.

In terms of how Christians see the world, it's a very bad way to choose who to vote for (as we shall see later).

In terms of how the secular public see Christians, it is an even more disastrous situation, because single-issue politics can easily be seen as the way that Christians think.

It was people who had gained such an impression who made comments to us when we started campaigning as the Christian Peoples Alliance, and who make similar comments to other Christian-labelled political movements. Give yourself a name like 'Christian Peoples Alliance', or write a book called *How Would Jesus Vote?*, and you'll trigger the same reaction in many secular people. They'll assume that your only interests are preaching right-wing moral and ethical values, fundamentalism (understood in a variety of ways and rarely accurately), a right-of-centre political agenda and much more.

I have experienced this myself when interviewed by the BBC during a by-election in which the CPA endorsed a candidate. 'Your candidate is a pro-life activist, known for his opposition to human cloning. Like it or not, Mr Gidoomal, your party's going to be branded as the party of a single issue. You'll be perceived as running on a platform of right-wing fundamentalism. That's what you will be seen to be about.'

'That's what they said about us in the London Mayoral and Assembly elections,' I told them, and reminded them about the Fantasy Mayor web site poll that ran during the election campaign (it is currently still available on-line at www.fantasymayor.com, and still worth visiting). Visitors to the site were shown a list of issues and invited to give each one a rating showing how important that issue was to them. Then they were told the candidate whose policies most closely matched their own.

I was the only explicitly Christian candidate, standing as the candidate for an explicitly Christian-labelled party, though of course visitors to the site didn't know who I was until the end. But if the Fantasy Mayor vote had been the vote that counted, I would be Mayor of London by now. I emerged as the winner, and I expect many who took part in the poll were quite surprised to find that the candidate clos-est to their ideal manifesto was a Christian candidate. If they had been told the party I belonged to, and asked to guess from that how closely the Christian candidate's mani-festo would match their personal wish-list, they would probably, I'm sure, have assumed that I was a single-issue politician. It's a matter of how one sees things. I'm sure some voters were also taken aback when *Time Out* maga-zine, assessing what the mayoral candidates stood for, said that the CPA had 'comfortably the most radical manifesto', and the *Evening Standard* said that our commitment to 'the homeless, jobless and carless' made us look more radical than Labour.

On the other hand voters often asked me where I stood on their own particular single issue. 'Are you pro-life, or would you allow abortion?... Are you for Europe or against Europe?... Should we join the Euro currency? Depending on your answer to that, I will decide whether I give you the vote or not.' As a candidate I can tell you that the danger, when you are so often asked about a particular issue, is that you tend to become focused on that issue. It becomes a dominating theme in your thinking in a way it was not before, and before long you're in danger of becoming a sin-gle-issue politician when you never intended or wanted to be. Single-issue politics is created by both voters and candi-dates!

Balancing the Total Agenda

There is a problem, however. Suppose that you were deeply committed to a cause – let's say the pro-life, anti-abortion cause. So that for you it dominated all your thinking, and all politics was overshadowed by it. Yes, it would be a single issue, that to you was immensely important. You would rather do anything than vote into power a party whose manifesto included a pledge to liberalise abortion law, and you would prefer to give your vote to a candidate who had a strong position on pro-life issues.

At the same time you recognise the danger of single-issue politics. You recognise that though there is one issue that is for you of supreme importance, politicians do a lot more than talk ethics all the time. They make decisions and cast votes in parliament on a huge range of issues, which, though not so important to you as your major concern, still affect the lives and well-being of millions of people. So how do you evaluate a candidate? If you vote for somebody who doesn't share your view – that the government should not legislate for abortion on demand, and that abortion, if it happens at all, should be an extremely unusual occurrence rather than the regular and frequent thing it is today – what will be the result? If you do not vote for a pro-life candidate, what options are there for you to get your pro-life concerns translated into political action?

It's a very common problem, and there are various ways of dealing with it. Here's one. My colleague David Porter lives in a southern constituency, a very safe Conservative seat. The sitting MP has held it for many years and it would take a political shift of seismic proportions for him to lose it.

David does not share his MP's views on a number of issues. From time to time the other parties put forward candidates to give them useful experience of the hustings. Sometimes these candidates present a package of policies that reflects David's chief concerns much more closely than do those of the sitting MP. So should he vote for one of the other candidates, as a practical commitment to the policies he wants to see followed?

There are two issues here. First, the rights of the sitting MP. Though David is not a Conservative voter by inclination, the MP is a good constituency MP who has in local issues done everything a local MP could be expected to do. David is impressed by the way he answers letters on ethical issues such as votes in the pro-life debate: even though the MP usually explains that he will be voting differently to David's preference, it's clear that he has considered the letter and the reply is not a rubber-stamp throwaway. This does not advance David's cause but does indicate an effective constituency MP. The first issue, therefore, is whether an MP doing the job more than adequately ought to be voted out because of his views on one, single, issue, and whether replacing him with a new and inexperienced MP who got your vote purely because he gave the right answer to one, single, question is a responsible use of a democratic vote.

This is not at all the only approach and it can't be applied to all situations. What would change David's situation, for example, would be if the Conservative party adopted policies for which he could not vote, which would immediately mean he couldn't vote for the sitting MP any more. But there will be some cases, and one of them might be yours, when the sitting MP has earned your vote even if you have some fundamental disagreements with him or her.

The second issue is that electing an MP who agrees with you on an issue isn't necessarily the only way of getting your views on that issue represented in Parliament. On most ethical and moral issues there are other MPs who are likely to agree with you and will be fighting for your cause. Some of them are involved in pressure groups like the Movement for Christian Democracy, CARE, or the Evangelical Alliance, which you or your church can join. Others are involved in societies or associations and you may be eligible to become a member or receive a newsletter. And you can write letters of support to other MPs, you can campaign in the press, you can lobby ministers, you can do a great many things. Not having a local MP who is on your side in an issue does not mean that your democratic voice can't be heard, even in Westminster itself. Sometimes it works well if you vote for the candidate who seems the best constituency MP and then look for other ways to pursue your own agenda.

Politics is about ordering and deciding priorities. Certainly from the politician's point of view, for MPs represent communities, and large numbers of the people in those communities voted for other candidates. The MP is responsible to all of them. But politics is about ordering and deciding priorities from the electorate's point of view too.

Voting means balancing your total agenda.

I think we need to have our perspectives opened up and broadened. After several decades in which Jesus' followers have done sterling work campaigning for single issues, we need to move on. If all we care about is one issue, even if it's a very important and fundamental issue about which it's right to be passionate, there's a real danger that all the other issues will begin to seem unimportant. What about unemployed people? What about disabled people? What about all the marginalised communities? There is a whole range of issues concerned with the society we live in: roads, trains, transport, schools and education.

There was once a prominent scholar who was an authority on the works of John Bunyan. His particular expertise was in Bunyan's minor works. There are around sixty of them and very few people have ever read them. The scholar became a roving evangelist for the minor works, giving talks and telling his audiences that they should all be reading the innumerable tracts and transcribed sermons that fill the pages of the Complete Works of Bunyan. He promoted his cause so enthusiastically that he became known as 'Mr Lesser-Known-Bunyan'. For him, Bunyan's great works like *The Pilgrim's Progress* didn't exist. He was an enthusiast for the lesser works. They were his single issue.

We have to learn to handle a multiplicity of issues, rather than become absorbed in single-issue politics. Admittedly there's a sense in which single-issue politics is really a large collection of single issues, but voting is about recognising which issue is the most important for you – and then determining the extent to which you are able to balance that with the other issues.

There are some extreme fundamentalists who say, 'No: the only thing in the world that matters is that which to me is the most important issue'. Such people will never be satisfied until they find a candidate who agrees with them on their single issue. But that isn't Christian voting, it isn't biblical voting, and it isn't how Jesus would vote. We have already seen his attitude to money (p. 27), and the contexts in which he viewed money and its effects: he opened up the issue and looked at it from several angles.

How Would Jesus Vote?

I believe that the whole New Testament shows that Jesus was not a single-issue thinker. He was a man with a single agenda, which was nothing less than the redemption of the world: but that agenda was a portfolio of many separate agendas all harnessed to make the whole agenda a reality.

The eighteenth-century preacher George Whitefield was once asked, 'Mr Whitefield, why is it that you continue to tell us, over and over again, "You must be born again"?'

'Because,' Whitefield replied, 'you must.'

For Whitefield the conversion of the lost was his greatest priority, the single issue that dominated his ministry. It was the single issue that drove all the preachers of the Evangelical Revival, of which Whitefield and John and Charles Wesley were leading figures. But the Evangelical Revival was concerned with more than people's souls. John Wesley, for example, was a powerful preacher and pastor, but he was also a forceful social campaigner and a driving force for education. He was a defender of the rights of the poor and underprivileged and an outspoken critic of the high-born and wealthy, if he disapproved of the way they lived – as the famous dandy, Beau Brummell, found to his cost. His name is mentioned in histories of education as well as in histories of the Church. For Wesley, that single issue of the redemption of the world was inseparable from the dignity and worth of individuals and the right of the dis-advantaged and vulnerable to be protected and fulfilled as people created in the image of God.

When Jesus began his ministry, John the Baptist was in prison. He sent his followers to Jesus to ask him a question: 'Are you the one who was to come, or should we expect someone else?' Jesus validated his ministry with a compre-hensive agenda: 'Go back and report to John what you hear and see: The blind receive sight, the lame walk, those who have leprosy are cured, the deaf hear, the dead are raised, and the good news is preached to the poor. Blessed is the man who does not fall away on account of me' (Matthew 11:4–6).

Single issues concern more than a single issue. As Christian photographer Sylvester Jacobs once remarked: 'There are more ways of shouting Jesus than shouting Jesus'. Whole agendas of social justice and reconciliation are involved. From those agendas the six principles we have already looked at derive, but they do not apply to a single issue: they apply to every issue.

So let me sum up the main question again. There is a learning process that we all need to engage in. How do we learn to be discerning? How do we discerningly examine manifestos and candidates on a wider basis than the single issue that might be important to them or to us – while at the same time not ignoring the fact that it isn't wrong to be passionate about a single issue? But there is more than one issue that is important.

The Person for the Job

> The last temptation is the greatest treason:
> To do the right deed for the wrong reason.[36]

So said Archbishop Thomas à Becket in T. S. Eliot's play, *Murder in the Cathedral*. And there are many examples of doing the right thing for the wrong reason in politics. Some politicians are notorious for adopting whatever views or policies they think will get them elected – only to behave very differently when in power. Fortunately it doesn't happen very often in Britain, probably because four years is not a long time to wait before retribution comes! Others pick their policies with popularity in mind and are quite happy to pursue them if they lead to election. And others campaign on policies without having thought them through or without having a deep commitment to them, so that in a sense they blunder into a position that is very acceptable to a great many voters.

So a voter might well find him or herself considering the candidacy of somebody who is, as far as he or she is concerned, saying the 'right' things, but their motives seem suspect.

In that situation, it's very important to know as much about the candidate as one can, and to try to find out if the policy being promised is likely to be translated into action if the candidate is elected, whatever the motives for adopting it might be. After all, if I needed my appendix removing, the first question I would ask of the surgeon is not 'Are you a born-again believer?' but 'Do you know how to remove an appendix?' If the answer to both questions is 'Yes', that's the ideal position to be in. If not, it's clear what the best choice is. I would rather have an atheist surgeon who is brilliant at his job than a Christian surgeon who was incompetent. That's admittedly rather an extreme case – but the principle is a good one.

Of course motives are important. But at the end of the day what really matters is delivery. When I look at manifestos and candidates what I am looking for is the promise to deliver what is closest to what I believe society needs. That is my criterion for choosing a candidate and it's what I expect of the government of the day. Of course, that means that I have to do something too: I have to listen carefully to the government, monitoring what is happening, checking as far as is practical that the means by which the promise is being delivered are legitimate and within the beliefs and practices and ethics that I hold. There will be another election in due course, and I will want to check promises against past performance as I decide how to cast my vote then. I'm not suggesting that we should all become political observers, browsing yesterday's Hansard over the breakfast table and buying every White Paper that the Government publishes. But Christianity is not just about wisdom in voting. It is also about holding government accountable.

If the promises are delivered, but we suspect the motives are wrong or even naive, who are we to judge? There is no good biblical ground for believing that somebody who does not look at things the way we do, or who does not wear the badge of our little group, is therefore dangerous.

Jesus taught this when his disciples came to him indignantly one day: "'Master," said John, "we saw a man driving out demons in your name and we tried to stop him, because he is not one of us."

"Do not stop him," Jesus said, "for whoever is not against you is for you"' (Luke 9:49–50). And the apostle Paul made a similar point, when he heard that Christians were dividing into two camps. There were those who had been converted by Paul's ministry, there were those who had been converted by the ministry of Apollos. 'What, after all, is Apollos? And what is Paul? Only servants, through whom you came to believe – as the Lord has assigned to each his task. I planted the seed, Apollos watered it, but God made it grow. So neither he who plants nor he who waters is anything, but only God, who makes things grow' (1 Corinthians 2:5–7).

The Big Picture: and Putting it All into Practice

So I would urge you to look at the big picture. Single-issue programmes like those of Whitefield and indeed of Jesus himself are umbrella programmes that bring together a wide range of other issues. Effectively carrying out a single-issue programme means being effective in the other issues as well. If a politician is absolutely rigorous and deeply committed to a single issue, but has no particular policy on the spectrum of other issues, he or she won't even be promoting the single issue effectively.

How do we put these thoughts into practice?

Let's stay with the same example, that of pro-life politics. Suppose that this is a matter of very major concern to you.

One day, during the run-up to an election, a candidate appears at your door canvassing. You've already seen her manifesto. In large letters it proclaims her to be a supporter of the pro-life movement. So far as issues like abortion and euthanasia are concerned she's an ideal candidate. But how exactly, there on your door step, can you determine whether she is the candidate who should receive your vote?

Once again, I can't give you a one-size-fits-all recipe. You and I are different people. No two candidates or campaigns are the same. But here's one way of approaching the situation that I hope puts into practice the essence of what we have discussed together in this book.

To start with, try not to evaluate any candidate in isolation. You're picking from a list of candidates, so you need to have an idea of the various possibilities the list contains. One useful method would be to use the material in Chapter 3 of this book – the Six Principles – to draw up a list of issues on which you want to know the candidates' views, and to use it as a check-list to compare the candidates in your ward or constituency.

When the candidate announces her pro-life position, it's tempting to spend all the time she has available sharing your common concern. But it's more useful to have your checklist in mind and find out what she thinks about other issues. You don't need to cross-examine her on abortion because you know the pro-life position already. But what is her policy on housing unmarried mothers?

Hopefully by the end of the conversation you will have a good idea of the candidate's policies across the board.

Try to do the same with every candidate who knocks at your door. For example, the man with the excellent track record in business: in his hands economic matters would be capably looked after. As a back-bencher, or district councillor, or parish councillor he would be sure to ask the questions and demand the kind of accountability that would be in my, and my neighbours', best interests. But ask him exactly how he intends to implement his financial policies, or those of his party. What is his policy on sleaze, or the cost of putting his economic plans into action? As a good businessman he might have very effective methods, but maybe they depend on rather dubious moral and ethical principles.

Personally, I would also want to ask this candidate what his views were on the National Health Service. As an NHS Trustee myself I know that the service needs competent financial management and that as a good businessman he would be able to deliver that. But what if he is the candidate of a party that has a policy on health that I feel is unbiblical? To what extent will the party policy overrule the candidate's wishes and plans for the constituency? Will local issues be subordinate to the national policy? How far will the candidate's promises be delivered in the local community?

The checklist approach is an effective one because it isn't designed to award marks – you have to recognise that nobody can be good at everything – but to help you choose a candidate who has a range of policies that support his key issue campaign.

I must confess that this approach to candidates and manifestos only sharpened in my own mind when I became a candidate myself. I realised that the voters who were stretching me most and forcing me to articulate my position were the people who asked me about things that weren't major topics in my manifesto. 'What did I think about the Euro?' I was asked many times, each time with a slightly different emphasis and from a slightly different perspective.

The Euro isn't really a London issue – and yet it is, for London is a world financial centre. I wasn't making policy on the hoof, but I *was* having to articulate positions and opinions that I had never had to articulate publicly before. And I knew that I was being judged by the questioner not only for my views on the Euro but also for what those views said about my position on wider issues.

Let me explain what I mean. I believe that in future elections, and possibly the next election, the battleground will be the question of whether we stay in Europe or get out. It will become, if not a single-issue topic, then certainly a very dominant one in electoral campaigning. As a Christian I believe that the issue should be discussed in a wider context. What do we as a nation think about community anyway? What, for example, is our policy on excluded communities? These are issues that hurt, on the ground, in the real world: what are we going to do about the poor, those who are the victims of unequal access to health care, those who are the victims of traffic discrimination in rural communities, those disabled people who are deprived of basic civil and human rights?

The issue of Europe embraces all these areas because almost every issue embraces them. And we need to say to candidates and parties at election time that government is about more than just whether we are in or out of Europe. Government is about jobs, inclusion, regeneration in deprived communities, building community, sharing prosperity. Those are issues that are applicable to a London Mayoral campaign and equally applicable to elections for the country at large. The European issue is the tip of a large iceberg, the bulk of which is how we build society and how we share prosperity.

So looking at canvassing both as a voter and as a campaigner, I am convinced that deciding where to cast one's vote is actually a considerable undertaking. It doesn't require a degree in political science but it does require thoughtful evaluating and comparison of different candidates' manifestos.

Party or Candidate?

There is an underlying question in all we have been discussing in this section, and it needs to be answered before we conclude.

Should we vote for the person who is standing for election, or the party he or she represents?

It seems to me that this question reflects the great advantage of democracy. We need to look both at the candidate and at the party. A party candidate's manifesto will be substantially the same as every other candidate's manifesto who represents that party. But if the candidate is worth voting for at all, there will be a part of the manifesto that is unique to local issues and sets forth the candidate's proposals for dealing with local problems and situations. And we need to examine both; it's a balance between the two.

For example, a candidate might say that he disagrees with his party about Clause 28,[37] saying that he or she would like to see it maintained in all local schools. But in a political landscape which is tending to become more centrist all the time, issues like Clause 28 are becoming the distinctives that separate candidates who otherwise would increasingly be looking like each other. And I believe that we may have to choose on that basis, selecting the candidate whose personal views most reflect what we want, irrespective of the views of the national party; and that we should trust that God will over-rule and make the voices of individuals count in changing party policy. And it may mean that we change the voting habits of a lifetime because the candidate for a different party from the one we normally vote for has expressed views that, if implemented, would make our wishes a reality.

That might sound hopelessly idealistic. Some diehards will certainly say, 'Once a Labour voter, always a Labour voter – I'll never vote Tory!' (and vice versa).

But that is what I am pleading for in this book: the vision that things can and do change. If, as I have suggested, voting demands substantial thought, then let's think why we are voting, rather than vote blindly on old traditional party lines. Let's ask instead, as we approach any election: How would Jesus vote?

The world changes all the time. Political parties change. As we finish writing this book in January 2001, the next General Election is widely believed to be just a few months away. Once we had Old Labour, now we have New Labour. The Conservative Party has transformed itself after its massive defeat in the last election. The Lib-Dems are a different party after four years of close association with government. The way we voted ten years ago is irrelevant to the present situation. So what is the new situation? What values have changed? How does the new situation square with my conscience? Even in the four years since the last general election, what now should I do with my vote?

Why Bother?

'I would vote for you,' the voter said to me regretfully. 'But what's the point? You're not going to get in, and if I vote Tory or Lib-Dem – well, there's a lot of Christians in those parties. I think I'll vote for them because I really think voting for you – though I really like your manifesto – is a waste of a vote, isn't it?'

I had too many conversations like that while I was campaigning. It's a very real fear that many voters have, and I want to end this book by considering the issue. Why bother?

The first answer, surely, is that every vote counts. There must be a large number of voters in the State of Florida who now regret not bothering to vote in the 2000 presidential election, which came down to counting votes by the hundred rather than the thousand.

But what if you were voting not for George Bush or Al Gore, but for a minority party candidate with no hope of election? What point is there then in voting?

Let me suggest three reasons why, if you want to vote for a small party, your vote is not wasted.

By-elections

In by-elections, small parties have the opportunity to develop an electoral base, to present their policies, and to make themselves known to the public. They get a degree of media exposure, they can work with local supporters (the CPA has had good support from churches, for example), and because they often field local candidates they can make a much bigger impact on local opinion than candidates who lost their seats at the last General Election and are standing in the by-election to get back into Parliament.

In a sense by-elections are training grounds for minor party candidates, but they are much more than that. If you vote for a minor party you are not wasting your vote and you may be contributing to the future growth and success of the party you vote for. Jesus, whose political opinions favoured the weak and powerless and who was rigorous in his scrutiny of the powerful and influential, would certainly have looked very carefully at the opportunities by-elections present.

Tactical Voting

Small parties often gain votes when a major party, particularly the party in government, is out of favour. 'Tactical voting' is often used as a means of punishing ineffective or unpopular governments, and it's not uncommon to find that small party candidates find themselves as MPs because the voters want to 'send a message' to the government. Of course the MPs rarely survive the next general election, for the constituency, having made its point, usually goes back to its usual habits.

But it doesn't always happen that way. What happened in Tatton in 1997 was largely tactical voting, and many local residents who were members of major parties warned Martin Bell that he was only keeping the seat warm until the next General Election. But Bell has proved an industrious and effective MP and, as we have already seen, intends to stand in the next general election. So the Martin Bell one-man 'Anti-Sleaze Party' has actually gained a seat which it might retain in the general election, on the basis of tactical voting – and has sent a message of earthquake proportions to the major parties! But even if the party you vote tactically for does not hold on to its seat, you have helped to have its views represented in Parliament for a time, and you have certainly improved its chances in the next election.

I'm sure that Jesus, who was well aware that his ministry was reaching the ears of the powerful and that he would soon be in direct confrontation with government, would appreciate the force of the messages that tactical voting can send!

Proportional Representation

I have left until last the most significant development of all in small-party politics: proportional representation.

Proportional representation (PR) is a simple principle. The *Encyclopaedia Britannica*'s definition is useful:

> An electoral device that seeks to create a representative body that reflects the distribution of opinion in the electorate.

PR ensures that minority groups will be represented in proportion to their numbers, whereas majority or 'first-past-the-post' systems (such as are used in UK parliamentary elections) reward strong parties and penalise weak ones by allowing the whole constituency or country to be represented by a candidate who may have received half or less of the votes.[38] It is a system that transforms the value of a vote.

There are various ways of implementing PR, and the details can be complex. Rather than attempt a summary (most general encyclopaedias and other reference books set out the various ways of implementing PR and explain the sometimes complex calculations involved), let me make one last reference to the CPA London campaign.

I am still a businessman, I am neither Mayor of London nor a member of the Assembly. Does that mean that the people who voted for me wasted their vote? Not at all.

First, the fact we did not gain an Assembly seat was due to a quirk of the version of PR used in the election: a threshold device, which set a further target candidates had to achieve over and above the proportional target set by the d'Hondt system of counting PR votes. We just failed to reach the threshold. The Evening Standard's Diary column called it a 'seatless victory'. This 'victory' actually sent a strong message to future election organisers. An independent body, the Electoral Reform Society, recommended after the election that the law should be changed regarding thresholds: it was unjust that the CPA won more votes in the count than the Conservative who was elected to the eleventh 'top-up' seat,[39] yet was not represented in the Assembly.

Here's a parallel example. If the CPA had gained the same result in Stormont (where there is no threshold) the party would probably have won four seats.

So the performance was very strong and showed up failings in the system that could well be changed because of our campaign. The votes were not wasted, even though they couldn't be turned into the result we hoped for, and the repercussions of that election and our campaign are still making waves in all sorts of places.

Second, the support that the CPA received was a crucial factor in the party's decision to continue. In 100 days, 100 members won the support of 100,000 people. It is an extremely encouraging basis for the future, given that most voters had never heard of the CPA before the campaign, and the CPA was the first party to urge Christians to vote for them not just because the party had Christ in the name, but on the grounds of the policies being put forward. Votes cast did not secure seats, but they did ensure that the CPA was acknowledged as a force to be reckoned with in British politics.

There is another advantage of the voting system used for London's mayoral election. It gave voters more than one vote; there were first and second preference votes, and both could be made to count if you understood how PR votes are counted.

The count proceeds in a number of 'rounds'. Because only the top-scoring candidates (usually two) in the first round qualify for the second, voters wishing to encourage minor party candidates should be encouraged to give their first preference vote to the minor party. The second preference vote could be for the majority party of their choice. In the second round, it is likely that their vote will count in the run-off between the top two candidates. This holds especially true in countries like the UK and the USA with two main parties and many minority parties.

In the London Mayoral elections, some of my supporters misunderstood how PR works. They wanted to encourage me, and they wanted to support a majority party candidate. So they gave me their second preference vote, and kept their first preference vote for the majority party candidate. This meant, however, that they lost the opportunity to send out a stronger signal by increasing my share of the first vote, and at the same time of helping their majority party candidate in the second round.

There is no doubt that the increasing role of PR in British elections will be a major factor in increasing the value of votes and the opportunities for small parties to make their voices heard.

The new electoral systems are transforming British politics. Coalition government now exists in Cardiff and Edinburgh (where, at the time of writing, Labour are in coalition with the Liberal Democrats). The fact that there is now a power-sharing Executive at Stormont, made possible by PR, underlines the point that electoral systems can oblige otherwise combative politics to become more about a search for conciliation and agreement. PR looks set to stay in British politics, with future Regional Assemblies such as in the North-West and North-East of England likely to be elected under PR and pressure coming from across the political spectrum for a 'Senate' elected by PR taking the place of the House of Lords. PR at local level would also end the 'one-party' fiefdoms so common in many local authorities.

A just representation of what people actually want – limiting of the power of the mighty parties – opening up the way for the weak and unrepresented to have their say – making people's choices matter –

Would Jesus approve of PR? I think so!

Conclusion

There is no one party or candidate for whom every follower of Jesus should vote, but voting, I passionately believe, is a Christian duty and privilege. Voting matters, and we have ample evidence in the Bible that in our voting, as in everything else, it is possible to bring to bear the mind of Jesus himself. We are fortunate to live at a time in history when we enjoy many freedoms, and the right to have a say in the governing of our nation is perhaps one of the greatest. We are even more fortunate that we do not have to carry out this awesome responsibility on our own.

Notes

34. Quoted in David Porter, *Mother Teresa: The Early Years* (SPCK, 1986), p. 98.

35. Harry Blamires, *The Christian Mind* (SPCK, 1963), pp. 3–4.

36. T. S. Eliot, *Murder in the Cathedral* (1935), Part I.

37. Clause 28 of the 1988 Local Government Act banned the use of local council funds to promote gay and lesbian lifestyles. Clause 28 was introduced by Margaret Thatcher's government after concerns that literature promoting homosexuality was being distributed in the nation's schools. The Clause has been a campaigning issue in the homosexual communities, its repeal is an important plank of New Labour policy, and its retention has been the subject of strong representations by religious and moral pressure groups.

38. See 'Proportional representation', *Encyclopaedia Britannica 1999 Multimedia Edition* (1999).

39. Top-up seats were awarded according to proportionate votes cast after the allocation of fourteen first-past-the-post seats. Ram qualified for the eleventh seat not because of the votes he received as mayoral candidate but because he was placed first on the CPA 'top-up' list.

Appendix 1

Would Jesus Vote?

Throughout history there have been groups of Christians who have shunned politics. Some, for example, have argued that believers live according to a higher law and shouldn't involve themselves in the affairs of unregenerate men and women and the systems they create to order their lives. Some have questioned how a follower of Jesus could possibly consider being part of a secular political party, which would include non-Christians and propose laws that would cater for non-Christian tastes and impose lesser standards of ethics and morals than the Bible sets out. Some have said that the Church and its priesthood should govern the country; and if the country doesn't agree, they opt out. Some have seen politics as the regulating system of all that they regard as fallen and unspiritual, and have become desert mystics, reclusives, hermits and solitaries. Some have argued that Christians have too much to do: entrusted with the Great Commission to take God's message to the whole world, politics is a distraction.

Would Jesus vote? The question really means, 'Does Jesus think his followers should have anything to do with secular politics?' Voting in elections is the way that democratic politics works: politicians represent the people, and the politicians are chosen by the votes of the people. So if Jesus considered politics to be a legitimate sphere of his followers' lives, he would endorse voting.

That leaves just two questions. First, would Jesus approve of politics as a human activity? And second, would Jesus vote and thereby teach that his followers should also vote? In other words, even if politics is acceptable as part of everyday life, is it something Christians should have anything to do with?

The Christian and the State

The biblical case that governments are legitimate earthly institutions rests on several passages, which we can only briefly look at here.

Mark 12

> Later they sent some of the Pharisees and Herodians to Jesus to catch him in his words. They came to him and said, 'Teacher, we know you are a man of integrity. You aren't swayed by men, because you pay no attention to who they are; but you teach the way of God in accordance with the truth. Is it right to pay taxes to Caesar or not? Should we pay or shouldn't we?'
>
> But Jesus knew their hypocrisy. 'Why are you trying to trap me?' he asked. 'Bring me a denarius and let me look at it.' They brought the coin, and he asked them, 'Whose portrait is this? And whose inscription?'
>
> 'Caesar's,' they replied.
>
> Then Jesus said to them, 'Give to Caesar what is Caesar's and to God what is God's.' (Mark 12:13–17)

This is the passage I referred to in Chapter 1, the trick question that Jesus spotted and turned back on his hearers. His point was that the state has a right to collect taxes to fund its policies, and he refused to denounce the state even though he and all his listeners had suffered under the harsh rule of the Romans.

It's important to notice, however, that Jesus was affirming the legitimacy of governments, not giving approval to the harshness and fallibility of the Roman oppressors. Two chapters earlier, in Mark 10, we read what Jesus thought of the behaviour of the government of the day. Sometimes Christians have taken from Mark 12 the principle that it is wrong to be critical of the government. The passage doesn't justify that interpretation, and if Jesus had thought it did, he would never have voted, because taking part in an election gives assent to the notion that government is answerable to the people.

Romans 13

> Everyone must submit himself to the governing authorities, for there is no authority except that which God has established. The authorities that exist have been established by God. Consequently, he who rebels against the authority is rebelling against what God has instituted, and those who do so will bring judgment on themselves. For rulers hold no terror for those who do right, but for those who do wrong. Do you want to be free from fear of the one in authority? Then do what is right and he will commend you. For he is God's servant to do you good. But if you do wrong, be afraid, for he does not bear the sword for nothing. He is God's servant, an agent of wrath to bring punishment on the wrongdoer. Therefore, it is necessary to submit to the authorities, not only because of possible punishment but also because of conscience. This is also why you pay taxes, for the authorities are God's servants, who give their full time to governing. Give everyone what you owe him: If you owe taxes, pay

taxes; if revenue, then revenue; if respect, then respect; if honour, then honour. (Romans 13:1–7)

If Mark 12 could be interpreted to mean that Christians should give unquestioning obedience to the state, Romans 13 could be taken in much the same way. But there are passages in the Bible that clearly say the opposite, for example Acts 17:6–7. And Jesus himself made it clear on several occasions that he did not regard himself as bound to obey the authorities unquestioningly.

The key to this passage is its teaching that governments are agents of God and have a God-given role. So citizens must co-operate with governments and obey them. But, just as in Mark 12, that doesn't mean that however badly a government rules, and however far it departs from God's purpose for society, it must be mindlessly obeyed. The theologian Manfred Brauch has suggested that rulers are part of God's plan for bringing about his intent of harmony and order in community life. So when they depart from that plan, they lose the right to be obeyed.[40]

On the basis of this passage Jesus would certainly vote, but that would not prevent him from objecting to unjust rule and expressing his disapproval of bad governments.

1 Peter 2

Submit yourselves for the Lord's sake to every authority instituted among men: whether to the king, as the supreme authority, or to governors, who are sent by him to punish those who do wrong and to commend those who do right. (1 Peter 2:13–14)

When Peter wrote those words, Nero was probably the emperor of Rome. What are we to make of a call to obey authority, written when the ruler of the known world was a depraved dictator who was willing to burn his imperial city if it meant the Christian Church would get the blame? And how does the immorality of Nero's court square with the description of earthly rulers as God's moral watchdogs?

If that seems a remote scenario, consider how Russian Christians must have felt reading these words during the rule of Stalin, or German believers reading them while Hitler was in power. In what sense are these words to be binding on Christians?

Several commentators have suggested that this passage is really talking about Christian conduct. It is the authorities who set the rules of civil behaviour. Christians should be doubly careful to submit to any moral or ethical laws and regulations, because if they do not they will bring the name of Christ into disrepute and become known as immoral people. 'The Jews were especially hated and counted infamous for this reason,' observes John Calvin, 'because they were regarded on account of their perverseness as ungovernable.'[41] Even in the days of communism, when Christian ethics were as far from the state agenda as could be and religious freedom had almost disappeared, there were many regulations controlling everyday morality and behaviour. Frequently these were trivial and irksome and many citizens ignored them, but Christians taking Peter's words seriously would strive meticulously to obey the regulations. So it can be argued that Peter's words are not intended to establish the status of government but the duty of individual Christians.

Revelation 13 and 18

I won't quote these chapters, for reasons of space. But it's important to read them because they give us God's perspective on government. Often governments are unjust and unfair, and obeying them is frustrating and difficult.

Under some governments it is possible to become voluntarily redundant and thus make more money from state benefits than from your previous salary. Young people are often condemned to long-term unemployment, and government training schemes are sometimes seen as the government merely going through the motions and creating paper jobs. Some people come to retirement and find that the nest-egg they saved for all those years turns out to be worth a lot less than they thought it would.

What makes it worse is that those who cheat the system seem to be doing so well out of it! And in that situation a Christian might well be tempted to reject any idea of submitting to a government that has allowed such things to happen – and in some cases, has caused them.

It's not only a modern problem. In biblical times it was often the same. On every hand, in generation after generation there was corruption, graft, cruelty and immorality. Asaph, the Psalmist, recorded it in poetry:

> But as for me, my feet had almost slipped;
>   I had nearly lost my foothold.
> For I envied the arrogant
>   when I saw the prosperity of the wicked…
> This is what the wicked are like –
>   always carefree, they increase in wealth.
> Surely in vain I have kept my heart pure;
>   in vain have I washed my hands in innocence.
> All day long I have been plagued;
>   I have been punished every morning.
> If I had said, 'I will speak thus,'
>   I would have betrayed your children.[42]

For Asaph it all seemed too much, until he changed his perspective:

> When I tried to understand all this,
>   it was oppressive to me
> till I entered the sanctuary of God;
>   then I understood their final destiny.[43]

The doom of Revelation 13, which shows the state becoming a tool of Satan, and of Revelation 18, which portrays the destruction of the great city of Babylon, reminds us that states and governments do come under the judgement of God. The functions they are allowed to exercise they exercise by his forbearance, and in the perspective of history any injustices and immorality will not go unpunished.

From these few passages, we can see that the Bible does teach the legitimacy of earthly governments and even suggests that they exist as agents of God to bring about his purposes in the world. They do not hold that position without accountability, however, and Christians are accountable too for how they respond to the moral demands of government.

Biblically, government is not a delegated responsibility. God is intimately concerned with how the world runs and he holds governments accountable and finally brings them under judgement. A country like Albania, which under Enver Hoxha outlawed religion and created the world's first officially atheist state, still ruled its people because God allowed it to do so.

So should Christians have anything to do with politics?

The verses we have looked at, and many others that are also in the Bible, indicate 'Yes!' If governments are to discharge their God-given duty of furthering God's purposes, they need the involvement of people who know what God's purposes are. We need politicians who are followers of Jesus in the House of Commons, in the House of Lords, in the Scottish and Welsh Assemblies, in Stormont.

In God's good providence, they are there.

We need followers of Jesus in political parties, in local groups and party associations.

In God's good providence, they are there.

We need followers of Jesus in the media, in schools, in public service, in trade unions, in the civil service – anywhere where God's perspective can be contributed to the ongoing task of government.

In God's good providence, they are there too.

Not everybody can be involved in politics to that extent. Some have other responsibilities, or family commitments, or demanding jobs; some are just not politics people, and their gifts are in other areas. But everybody can vote. Indeed everybody *should* vote. As I said earlier, voting is the first plank of democratic politics. A vote may seem a small thing, but the most powerful democratic government only holds office because a majority of people did that small thing.

Would Jesus vote?

I am sure he would, for he believed in accountable government, and voting is the fundamental way of holding governments to account.

Notes

40. Manfred T. Brauch, *Hard Sayings of St Paul* (Hodder & Stoughton, 1990), pp. 82–84.

41. John Calvin, *On the First Epistle of Peter*, comment on 2:14.

42. Psalm 73:2–3,12–16.

43. Psalm 73:16–17.

Appendix 2

The Christian Peoples Alliance

The Christian Peoples Alliance developed from the Movement for Christian Democracy, following a consultation process with its members in Spring 1999, asking for responses to the idea of a party of Christian inspiration, within the Christian Democratic tradition. Discussions in Scotland, Wales and London and a questionnaire published in the MCD members' magazine led to a report concluding that there would be widespread support for an identifiably Christian party. That led to the setting up of the Christian Peoples Alliance and its launch in May 1999. The new party contested seats in the May 2000 London Mayoral and Assembly elections and in the November 2000 Preston by-election.

The CPA is not a breakaway from the MCD. It is an extension of its work. Many people are members of both. Its basis of operation is the same set of Six Guiding Principles that the MCD formulated, and these are the heart of its manifestos and discussion papers. A party rooted in the historic Christian faith, the CPA's faith and principles are drawn from the Bible, especially the life and teaching of Jesus Christ, as well as from Christian political insights down the centuries. We are also aware of Christian failure and injustice in the past.

Our aim is to follow and fulfil these principles in British political life:

- ❑ Respect for human life given by God.
- ❑ Careful economic stewardship of God's creation.
- ❑ Reconciliation among races, nations, religions, classes, gender and communities.
- ❑ Social justice to address wrongs and provide restitution to the wronged.
- ❑ Democracy which sees government as service, and practises accountability and truthfulness to the people and to God.
- ❑ Commitment to the fairness of markets and patterns of exchange.
- ❑ Resourcing and empowering the poor, to share with all.
- ❑ Peacemaking, opposing wars and the causes of wars.
- ❑ Respect for family, religion, education, the arts, business and other institutional areas in a society of limited government.
- ❑ Respect for God's law as the basis for a stable society.
- ❑ Direct compassion for those with needs.
- ❑ Open, tolerant government which subjects itself to debate and critique.

The CPA's information pack and membership details are available from:

Christian Peoples Alliance
PO Box 932
Sutton, Surrey
SM1 1HQ
website: www.cpalliance.net
email: info@cpalliance.net

Reading List

This is intended to be a starting point for further reading on some of the topics discussed in this book. It's intended not as a comprehensive guide to Christianity and politics, but as a selection of material that has been used in the book or which we have found helpful.

Alton, David, *What Kind of Country?* (Marshall Pickering, 1988)

Alton, David, *Faith in Britain* (Hodder & Stoughton, 1991)
Lord Alton is a founding figure in modern British Christian Democracy. These books set out his political credo and much of the background of Christian Democracy.

Blamires, Harry, *The Christian Mind* (SPCK, 1963). This is the book that brought Blamires, already a writer on literary and Christian themes, to widespread public attention. His thesis, which is argued with grace and an acerbic wit, has become no less relevant since publication.

Fogarty, Michael, *Christian Democracy in Western Europe,* 1820-1953 (Routledge & Kegan Paul, 1957).

Fogarty, Michael, *Motorways Merge* (Christian Democrat Press, 1999).

Professor Fogarty, President of the Movement for Christian Democracy until his death in January 2001, provides seminal historical analysis and assessment of the development of Christian Democracy.

Gidoomal, Ram, with Mike Fearon, *Sari 'n' Chips* (Monarch, 1993). This book provides some useful information on Ram's background.

John Paul II, *Encyclical Letter Centesimus Annus* (Catholic Truth Society, 1991). This short document provides a Roman Catholic perspective on many of the issues we have discussed. We have chosen this particular Encyclical because it was written in the aftermath of the revolutions of 1989-1990.

Porter, David, *Back to Basics: the Anatomy of a Slogan* (OM Publishing, 1994). A study, prompted by John Major's ill-fated slogan, of the application of Christian ethics and moral principles to government and public policy.

Stott, John R. W., *Issues Facing Christians Today* (Marshalls, 1984)

Stott, John R. W., *The Contemporary Christian* (IVP, 1992)

Stott, a leading evangelical commentator, sets issues of politics and government against the whole spectrum of human life and demonstrates the validity of Christian belief as a basis for analysis and action.

Temple, William, *Christianity and Social Order* (Penguin, 1942). A widely influential book of its time, Temple's essay has remained influential.